Keep Your Day Job

T0334230

As millennials and Gen Z grow their influence in the workplace, side hustling and overemployment are emerging from the dark corners of the corporate world—but many companies still resist this trend.

How can employees leverage the shifting power dynamic to build their own empires? Build now and ask forgiveness later: this book shows you how. Rich with insights from personal experience and doctoral research, this is the story of more than a decade of side hustling alongside successes, and failures, in a career in corporate America. But more importantly, it is a roadmap on how to successfully incorporate a side hustle into your life in a way that supports your day job too. Not everyone starts a side hustle to eventually quit their day job, and many individuals enjoy and take pride in the dual incomes they can earn this way. This book centers and prioritizes this path.

No matter their industry, this book will resonate with readers who have been burned by their side hustle (or fear that they might be), as well as HR professionals who want to support change in corporate America and leaders who value and prioritize innovation to impact their workforce for the better.

Dannie Lynn Fountain is a multipassionate human—by day, she's a disability accommodations program manager at Google and by night she supports clients and brands with HR-focused diversity, equity, and inclusion strategies. She is also the founder of the #SideHustleGal movement and the "original" Side Hustle Gal. Dannie Lynn has been interviewed or quoted in the *New York Times, Harvard Business Review, Forbes, Bustle, Bloomberg, Business Insider, Cosmopolitan, Digiday, The Everygirl, Girlboss,* and more.

Keep Your Day Job

Leverage Your Side Hustle To Grow Your Corporate Career, Regardless Of What HR Says You Can Do

Dannie Lynn Fountain

Routledge
Taylor & Francis Group

NEW YORK AND LONDON

Designed cover image: Getty

First published 2024
by Routledge
605 Third Avenue, New York, NY 10158

and by Routledge
4 Park Square, Milton Park, Abingdon, Oxon, OX14 4RN

Routledge is an imprint of the Taylor & Francis Group, an informa business

© 2024 Dannie Lynn Fountain

Library of Congress Cataloging-in-Publication Data
Names: Fountain, Dannie Lynn, author.
Title: Keep your day job : leverage your side hustle to grow your corporate career, regardless of what HR says you can do / Dannie Lynn Fountain.
Description: New York, NY : Routledge, 2024. | Includes bibliographical references and index. | Provided by publisher.
Identifiers: LCCN 2023057672 | ISBN 9781032689586 (hardback) | ISBN 9781032688022 (paperback) | ISBN 9781032689623 (ebook)
Subjects: LCSH: Supplementary employment. | Career development.
Classification: LCC HD5854.5 .F68 2024 | DDC 658.1/141—dc23/eng/20240116
LC record available at https://lccn.loc.gov/2023057672

ISBN: 978-1-032-68958-6 (hbk)
ISBN: 978-1-032-68802-2 (pbk)
ISBN: 978-1-032-68962-3 (ebk)

DOI: 10.4324/9781032689623

Typeset in Galliard
by Apex CoVantage, LLC

To Dr. Kevin Danley, for creating the community both of us needed in order to survive academia . . .

. . . and to the managers who fired me or PIP'ed me, my audacity raised yours and here we are.

Contents

Before You Read

Moonlighting, side hustling, and overemployment have long existed in the dark corners of corporate America—many employees leverage them for secondary income, stability, and thought leadership, even though companies would prefer that they didn't.

As corporate America becomes increasingly millennial-run and Gen Z–driven, the power dynamic is shifting and these forms of additional income are becoming less taboo.

So how do we capitalize on it? How do we as employees leverage this shift to "build our own empires," as explained by the online financial influencers?

We build now and ask forgiveness later.

I've been in corporate America for nearly a decade now and throughout that entire time, I've had a side hustle. I've been fired because of it, been promoted despite it, and leveraged it to land jobs where my corporate experience just wasn't enough. But throughout all that, it's been necessary for me to act first, build steadily, and check in with HR later. Corporations are risk averse—it's easier for them to say no up front than to monitor what you're building and hope for the best.

Keep Your Day Job is the story of more than a decade of side hustling alongside a successful career in corporate America and the failures that have come with it too. But more importantly, *Keep Your Day Job* is a roadmap on how to successfully incorporate a side hustle into your life in a way that supports your day job too. Not everyone starts a side hustle to eventually quit their day job—many individuals enjoy and take pride in the dual incomes they can earn this way. This book centers and prioritizes this path.

Readers of *Keep Your Day Job* will find community with others looking to craft an exit strategy—a backup plan for when corporate America decides they've had enough—or at the very least generate some supplemental income to tackle debt or chase some dreams.

This book is built on my doctoral degree capstone (can be downloaded at danniefountain.com/dba) and is backed by the rigorous academic standards of research that apply to doctoral-level writing.

But Why Me?

More than a decade ago, I was a high schooler with an itch to try something new, so I started my very first business. That business would carry me through the remainder of high school and all of college, offering me "side pocket money" and helping me build work experience before I graduated.

During my final undergrad internship, I would actually end up being fired due to this side hustle. The perceived threat of something successful that didn't make me beholden to the then-CEO of a small business complicated my ability to be successful in his eyes.

This back and forth of successful business but equally powerful threat continues to follow me today, a decade later. Now, I'm a 30-year-old heavily tattooed, plus-size, queer, sober, neurodivergent (autistic + ADHD), biracial woman in tech. And I have a side hustle that not only got me my job at Google but also provides me income stability and an additional feeling of safety. But it still threatens my career success too.

I'm not alone in this either—60% of Gen Z and 55% of millennials have side hustles too.[1] But not all of us have the freedom or safety to be bold in our business choices, because our corporate jobs don't quite understand how side hustles aren't a threat. In late 2022, I made an Instagram post sharing that less than 50% of my total income comes from my full-time employment at Google. Less than a month later, Google (among other tech companies) conducted a massive layoff sweep that prompted an outcry of Instagram DMs from other tech employees asking how to diversify their income too. The time is now for educating corporate employees on how critical it is to have multiple income streams—including a side hustle.

My education and my work at Google is the "current state" of a journey that started in high school. A boldness and recognition that nobody else was going to provide the life I wanted, I knew that I had to build it on my own. That first business snowballed into more work and more opportunity (through blood, sweat, and tears) and eventually became the entity you now know as Focused on People. At the same time, I've had a thriving career working in marketing and human resources for Fortune 500 companies like Whirlpool, H&R Block, and Google. And I've had that thriving career while being authentically myself every step of the way, including in how I approach my work.

Dannie Lynn Fountain

Note

1 https://zapier.com/blog/side-hustle-report-2022/.

Acknowledgments

This wasn't my first book, but it was perhaps the most personal. I'm known among my friend group for evangelizing the benefits of a side hustle and/or multiple streams of income and I'm thrilled to now have exerted that same peer pressure on you.

This book, and all of my writing projects, would be impossible without the contributions and support of so many humans—many more than I can capture here. I'm grateful to every single one of them for their contributions to this work and the general pursuit of meaningful acceptance of side hustling. I am certain there are folks I have missed in this acknowledgments section, know that I am profoundly grateful for your support and never for a moment believe that I underestimate your value in my life.

To my wife, Kaity. We did it again! I still cannot believe you said yes to writing another book and I am beyond grateful for your support. We knew better what we were getting into this time and yet you were still this book's number one champion even though my continued procrastination. *(On that note, ADHD, right? Strengths: Works well under pressure. Weaknesses: Doesn't work otherwise.)*

To my literary agent, Rachel Beck of Liza Dawson Associates, you continue to be an incredible support to my writing career and I would not be the author I am without you. Your advice, guidance, demystification of the publishing industry, and friendship have made this book (and all my traditionally published writing) what it is.

To the team at Routledge, thank you for loving this book as much as I do! It's a bit of a controversial take on the traditional entrepreneurial text, but I hope it ushers in a whole new era of side hustling. It's because of you that this book is out in the world!

To Dr. Kevin Danley, my doctoral advisor. The dedication says it all. Your guidance and mentorship, the doctoral writing that you helped shape, it all led here. Thank you.

To Dr. Vicki Baker, the OG side hustler. There is no one I have admired more greatly in the ways that you juggle everything on your professional and personal plate. You've inspired me in so many ways and it was your introduction that lit the spark to make this book possible.

To the small but mighty team behind the three LLCs that comprise my entrepreneurial pursuits, thank you for always being there. Thank you for supporting a girl with big dreams who always takes on too much and asks the world of you. You've made these big dreams possible.

As the dedication says, to the managers who fired me or PIP'ed me, my audacity raised yours and here we are. Thank you for lighting the fire that drove the career that led to this book.

To my friends, you know who you are. Thank you for absolutely everything, in every moment. And to my family, both blood and chosen. To Granny and Grampy, to Vickie and Evandro and Chris, to Jan, to Ginny and Cyndi, to Kayleigh and Lindsey and David, to Sarah and Taylor. Your strength in every moment of my life, no matter what it threw at us, made us stand deeper in love and taught us to prioritize what matters most.

And last but not least, to Briggs. My last traditionally published book was the first time my editor had seen a dog mentioned in the acknowledgments. We're here again, because you're the literal Emotional Support Animal who makes all this work possible. While you went to dog heaven before this book could be released, it wouldn't have been written without you.

Definitions to Norm On

1099 Economy. A network of gig workers and independent contractors that have income reported on a 1099-MISC or 1099-NEC (Oei, 2018).

Conflicts of Interest. Work that conflicts with the employee's core role functions at their place of full-time employment (Fröhlich et al., 2013).

Moonlighting. The voluntary delivery of services or the creation of goods outside of a daytime role in exchange for compensation (Saxon, 2015) and is synonymous with side hustle (Scott et al., 2020). Moonlighting is also holding a second job or participating in entrepreneurial work outside of a full-time role (Scott et al., 2020).

Side Hustle. Income-generating work performed alongside a full-time job (Sessions et al., 2021) and is often synonymous with moonlighting (Scott et al., 2020).

Technology Industry (US). This sector is a group of niche industries having high concentrations of STEM (science, technology, engineering, and math) knowledge workers (Johansson et al., 2019). Sample companies found within the United States technology industry include computer manufacturing, computer software, social media, and online communications platforms (Teti et al., 2019).

Part I

Foundational Knowledge

Chapter 1

What Exactly Is a Modern-Day Side Hustle?

Modern day side hustles take many forms and there is no one "true path" or right way to side hustle. That said, there are generally three broad categories to which this secondary work falls into. These categories are moonlighting, side hustling, and overemployment.

Moonlighting is not a new concept; the word has existed in the current context since the 1950s (Katz & Krueger, 2018). Generally speaking, moonlighting is a subset of side hustling that is pursued for the sole purpose of income generation and not necessarily to build some form of intellectual property.

The phrase **"side hustle"** has also existed in the American lexicon since the 1950s, and is generally defined as secondary employment that is either purely for income generation (i.e. moonlighting) or for the dual purpose of income generation and intellectual property development.

Overemployment is more clearly separated from the other two forms of secondary work. It is generally defined as the rising practice of holding two full time jobs at the same time, often completing both jobs remotely. An unintended side effect of the rise of remote work over the past couple years has been an increase in the ability to exploit the lack of oversight from management or simply maximize the inefficiency and bloat of corporate America. As the labor economy becomes increasingly tenuous, cashing in multiple paychecks from different companies helps protect against the risk of losing a job. This trend is increasingly prevalent in the technology industry, where the primary emphasis is on productivity and work output versus facetime or hours logged.

Throughout the remainder of this book, all three forms of secondary work will collectively be referred to as "side hustling," but it is understood that the side hustling experience can be customized to the pursuer's needs and goals.

DOI: 10.4324/9781032689623-2

Proliferation of Side Hustling

The 1099 economy, defined as the network of gig workers and independent contractors, in the United States has grown by 22% in recent years without a correlated decrease in W-2 forms. The W-2 economy meanwhile, defined as those working traditional employment and receiving W-2 tax forms, has actually declined by 3.5% during the same period. The consensus in business and academic research indicates that a vast number of full-time employees are turning to moonlighting for various reasons, but the allure of additional income remains the predominant one.

It's no secret that 60% of Gen Z and 55% of millennials have some form of the variations on a side hustle defined earlier.[1] But what is a secret—and what has yet to be fully explored—is how defined the line is between side hustles that advance your career and side hustles that present a true and valid conflict of interest with your day job. As side hustles become the norm in corporate America, it's time to unpack this, time to draw a line in the sand, and time to claim the power that comes from having a side hustle and what it can do for your career, regardless of what your employer thinks or wants.

This book tells stories of my own side hustle experiences—getting fired just because I have financial freedom outside of work, the ways in which cow-orkers and bosses have felt threatened by something that has no impact on them at all—and holds space for yours too. It seeks to define and understand what this "new economy" looks like—one where the majority of employees have side projects that not only provide them meaningful income but can also advance their careers in corporate America too. Finally, this book takes a hard look at exactly what a noncompete agreement is, how enforceable they actually are, and how to make risk-informed decisions for the ways in which you navigate your full time job.

What Can a Side Hustle Look Like?

Side hustles take many forms and to contextualize the remainder of this book, we must first generate a shared understanding of just how expansive the definition of side hustling truly is. What follows is a breakdown of my own side hustles and some real examples of how they show up in my life. To provide an anchor for the following percentages, my core full time job is 43% of my total annual income.

Seasonal Employment represents about 19% of my total annual income (equal to my core full time job if annualized). Seasonal employment is any work that is done on a recurring basis but only for a portion of the year. This can be anything from working at Target as a cashier during the holidays, working security at concert venues during peak summer season, or working remotely in any number of annual recurring roles such as bookkeeping, event management, or leasing. The advantage of seasonal employment is that the companies typically know they need the seasonal influx of labor on an annual basis and it is a short-term financial boost that becomes predictable year after year.

Entrepreneurship represents 32% of my total annual income and is a broad bucket including all of the self-employment activities I undertake in a given year. This includes the income generated from: consulting, public speaking, Instagram/social media, paid online content, book royalties (self and traditionally published), board memberships, and other miscellaneous smaller activities. This bucket ebbs and flows based on my own seasons of life, how much effort I dedicate to marketing myself and my services, and the needs of the industries I serve.

Resale Platforms represent 3% of my total annual income and include any goods that I resell on digital platforms or in person. In recent years, I have used: Poshmark, Mercari, PangoBooks, StillWhite, Facebook Marketplace, and my local used bookstore. Once the goods are listed on the digital platform, the income is largely passive, as the platforms are incentivized to drive traffic to the listings.

Semi-Passive Income represents 1.3% of my total annual income and is the most varied category within this list. Digital product sales are the longest-lasting subcategory. I've sold digital products on Etsy and my own website for more than a decade. Other components of this category include affiliate income, user research interviews/surveys, product and app-based rebates (Fetch, Ibotta, Aisle, etc.), and other miscellaneous online sources of income.

Group Fitness Coaching represents 1% of my total annual income (but if you include the cost of my now-free monthly membership, it grows to 2%). I joined a studio fitness gym and ended up also becoming a certified coach as well, where I now coach two to five classes/week.

Support Group Leader work represents less than 1% of my total annual income. I joined a community around a medical procedure I underwent and now serve as a support group leader within that community, leading two to three support groups per month.

Not represented here include less traditional forms of "income" that I also passively pursue, such as maximizing the interest on my high yield savings account, capitalizing on credit card sign up bonuses and redeemable offers, and maximizing employment benefits at both my core full-time and seasonal employment.

Looking at each of these categories gives an initial impression of different side hustles you could leverage or engage in. Other examples include real estate, gig work, becoming a tutor, launching a podcast or YouTube channel, dropshipping, selling photography on stock photo websites, or transcribing or translating audio or documents. Reading these examples might also help you see that you are already engaging in one or more side hustles without even realizing it!

Who Can Have a Side Hustle?

The short answer is "nearly anyone" but the longer more realistic answer is "anyone who has a sense of stability in life, the mental space to take on another project, and the legal ability to secure additional income." The prevailing assumption is that anyone with a laptop or tablet, a set of marketable skills, and access to the internet can engage in the proliferation of side hustles available today, however side hustles are only truly accessible to a much smaller subset of the population. Being aware of the restrictions and considerations in your own life is important to ensure that engaging in a side hustle will not endanger your current situation. For example, these are three more common situations that may preclude someone from building a side hustle:

Anyone receiving **Social Security Disability Income** is limited by an income cap and any income earned over that cap will reduce or eliminate entirely their SSDI payments. A colleague I know in the book influencer community is unable to monetize their platform the way that other bookish influencers do, because doing so would cause them to lose most or all of their SSDI income and medical insurance, which is critical to their ability to survive.

Similarly, anyone who is subject to the income caps of **Medicaid**. There are many reasons individuals will cap their income to remain on Medicaid, including considerations of cost of care for chronic illnesses. Many of those who have chronic illnesses will incur millions of dollars of medical bills a year and one of the only ways to avoid medical debt insolvency is to remain on Medicaid and thus be subject to the associated income caps.

Anyone with **significant caretaking responsibilities**, such as those individuals who are a member of the "sandwich generation." While this limitation is more personal than legal, there is only so much time in a day and so much energy a human can expend on the daily responsibilities they might have. If caretaking is absorbing the majority of someone's energy, their ability to have a side hustle is significantly diminished.

Understanding these foundational elements of side hustling—what subtypes exist, the diversity of styles or formats, and who may or may not be able to participate—is critical to understanding the remainder of this book and where you might choose to take action.

To Consider:

1. Am I precluded from side hustling for any reason?
2. What subtype of side hustle would I be interested in?
3. Do I want my side hustling to be a single format or an amalgamation of a few formats based on season or accessibility?

Note

1 https://zapier.com/blog/side-hustle-report-2022/.

Chapter 2

How Does Corporate America Restrict Side Work, and Is It Fair?

Seeing just how expansive the definition of a side hustle is can also help illuminate why employers are concerned about competitive activity, moonlighting, and the various agreements signed when beginning new employment.

Many industries today leverage hiring based on traits like intrapreneurship, which drove the desire for hiring employees who at that time had or in the future would have a willingness to moonlight alongside their full-time employment.[1] Hiring in this manner created a large employee base with a propensity for entrepreneurship without the company having stringent (or at least well-defined) policies to govern such activity.[2]

Beyond sharing of competitive information, the main concern for employers related to moonlighting is the spillover of full-time work to part-time work.[3] This concern posits that the distraction of moonlighting work reduces the productivity and focus of full-time work while also causing the side hustle to benefit from learnings and expenses paid for by the full-time employer.[4] This benefit is another layer of competition, as the full-time employer is indirectly paying for the development of the moonlighting activity's profitability and growth.[5]

State and Industry Specific Considerations

Specific to the technology industry, noncompete policies are a particularly nebulous issue due to the significant presence of technology company originations in California (Baron & Hannan, 2002). California largely does not accept noncompete agreements as the California Civil Code outlawed them in 1872.[6] This was reaffirmed in a legal battle in 2005 regarding the noncompete agreement of a former Microsoft employee hired at Google and a case in 2008 that declared even "narrowly drawn" noncompetes invalid. This enforcement regulation also applies to out-of-state noncompetes when applied to employees now working in California. The primary exclusion from California's noncompete ban is related to trade secrets, which are still

DOI: 10.4324/9781032689623-3

protected under state law, as seen in the Levandowski case between Uber and Waymo.[7]

Despite the unenforceability and impacts of California law, data shows that nearly half of all technical professionals in the United States have signed employment contracts complete with noncompete agreements.[8] The impact of these agreements leads to employees involuntarily exiting technical fields for a time to avoid litigation, however doing so dramatically impacts employee earning potential and therefore employee-employer relationships. While these barriers to mobility are intended to keep employees at a company, in practice, they increase tension between moonlighting employees and employers and lead to increased attrition.

While states like California have taken a hard line for decades on noncompete policies, many states do not have laws against these policies. However, in many cases, noncompete agreements are found to be unenforceable even without existing case law, such as in the case of Novo Nordisk.[9] Additionally, in July 2021, President Biden signed an executive order that is intended to prohibit unfairly restricting employee mobility (Exec. Order No. 14036, 2021). In doing so, the executive order works to eliminate situations like that of Jimmy Johns employees who leave the company and are prohibited from working for any other sandwich shop or at any location within two miles of a Jimmy Johns location.[10]

Since the 2021 executive order, additional states have joined the noncompete ban, including Colorado, Minnesota, North Dakota, and Oklahoma. Many of these laws have very narrow exceptions and essentially render noncompetes moot. In September 2023, California increased protections in its preexisting ban, including expanding access to attorneys for the purpose of challenging a ban. New York state has passed a ban on noncompetes in the legislature in June 2023 and that ban awaits signing by the New York state Governor.

Finally, even states that allow noncompete agreements have added restrictions to what is permitted. More than 20 states have carved out restrictions including income floors (no noncompetes for those who earn less than $100,000, as an example) or banning no-poach agreements (those that require nonsolicitation of former coworkers).

What Happens Now

While many companies have fully realized that their previous noncompete solutions may no longer be effective, there are alternatives that are still legal and being pursued. These alternatives include tighter confidentiality agreements, restrictions through "trade secret protection" laws, bonus structures tied to deterring "unwanted" behavior related to competitive activity, and increased activity in the area of information security.

Companies find themselves in a dichotomy where they have intentionally sought out employees with entrepreneurial skills for the purpose of workplace innovation and now no longer have as many legal options for those employees engaging more liberally in entrepreneurial activity. This may lead to an increase in scrutiny from HR departments on employees' extracurricular activity, or a decrease in "forgiveness not permission" mindsets towards thought leadership and other outside engagements.

Steps to Take

As you work on any side hustle activities, consider taking the following steps to ensure your activity is protected and in line with expectations even as legal agreements and enforceability continue to shift.

1. **Maintain confidentiality:** While noncompete agreements are shifting in enforceability, confidentiality and trade secret agreements continue to be upheld. Ensure that all activity complies with confidentiality clauses and your side hustle work does not share sensitive information or trade secrets. Tread carefully if your side hustle work engages with any of your employer's direct competitors.
2. **Document noncompeting activities:** Keep a record of activities and roles to aid you if competitive activity ever comes into question.
3. **Adhere to PR and other policies:** Specifically in the thought leadership space, if you are being interviewed or building thought leadership through media pieces or books, ensure that you carefully craft your language to avoid the appearance of "speaking on behalf of [your employer]."

To Consider:

1. Did I sign a noncompete agreement when I began employment at this company?
2. Do I understand the other policies at work that may impact my side hustle or other extracurricular activities?
3. Have I taken steps to ensure that my extracurricular activities are not perceived as competitive or in violation of other company policies?

Notes

1 Gawke, J. C., Gorgievski, M. J., & Bakker, A. B. (2018). Personal costs and benefits of employee intrapreneurship: Disentangling the employee intrapreneurship, well-being, and job performance relationship. *Journal of Occupational Health Psychology, 23*(4), 508–519. https://doi.org/10.1037/ocp0000105.
2 Gawke, J. C., Gorgievski, M. J., & Bakker, A. B. (2018).

3 Sessions, H., Nahrgang, J. D., Vaulont, M. J., Williams, R., & Bartels, A. L. (2021). Do the hustle! Empowerment from side-hustles and its effects on full-time work performance. *Academy of Management Journal, 64*(1), 235–264. https://doi.org/10.5465/amj.2018.0164.

4 Yang, L.-Q., Simon, L. S., Wang, L., & Zheng, X. (2016). To branch out or stay focused? Affective shifts differentially predict organizational citizenship behavior and task performance. *Journal of Applied Psychology, 101*(6), 831–845. https://doi.org/10.1037/apl0000088.

5 Yang, L.-Q., Simon, L. S., Wang, L., & Zheng, X. (2016).

6 Jackson, H. (2008, August 7). Calif. supreme court finds noncompete clauses invalid. *CNET.* https://www.cnet.com/news/calif-supreme-court-finds-non compete-clauses-invalid/.

7 Korosec, K., & Harris, M. (2020, August 4). Anthony Levandowski sentenced to 18 months in prison as new $4B lawsuit against Uber is filed. *TechCrunch.* https://techcrunch.com/2020/08/04/anthony-levandowski-sentenced-to-18-months-in-prison-as-new-4b-lawsuit-against-uber-is-filed/.

8 Marx, M. (2011). The firm strikes back: Non-compete agreements and the mobility of technical professionals. *American Sociological Review, 76*(5), 695–712. https://doi.org/10.1177/0003122411414822.

9 Moelis, J. (2020). 1st Circ. holds non-compete agreement unenforceable against fired and rehired employee. *National Law Review, XI*(227). https://www.natlaw review.com/article/1st-circ-holds-non-compete-agreement-unenforceable-against-fired-and-rehired.

10 Spiggle, T. (2021, July 16). President Biden's recent executive order takes aim at non-competes. *Forbes.* https://www.forbes.com/sites/tomspiggle/2021/07/16/president-bidens-recent-executive-order-takes-aim-at-non-competes/?sh=2 92505972cc4.

Chapter 3

Protecting Your Intellectual Property in and out of Work

Your intellectual property (IP) is one of your most critical assets and engaging in side hustling makes it even more critical to ensure that you are taking active steps to protect it.

It is likely that you signed an intellectual property agreement as a part of your onboarding, especially if you are a "knowledge worker" (workers whose main capital is knowledge). The primary purpose of these agreements is to clarify the ownership and rights related to IP created while employed at the organization. This IP can include inventions, designs, trademarks, trade secrets, and other creative works. Some companies also include carve-out provisions where you can specifically list IP created prior to employment that you explicitly want documented as set apart from your employment agreement.

In understanding the impact of IP agreements on your side hustle, it is important to first understand the scope of the document you might have signed.

Ownership of Work: It is common for IP agreements to state that any work created within the scope of employment (or during the time of employment) is considered the property of the employer. This traditionally would mean that any documents, innovations, designs, etc. created while employed are owned by the employer, but through the side hustle lens, could also mean that the employer might claim ownership of related side hustle work. For example: if your primary employment is as a graphic designer for H&M and on your own time, you create a t-shirt design that goes viral on TikTok and sells 50,000 units, your employer might try to claim that design as their IP as both your primary employment and side hustle involved graphic design and H&M does sell t-shirts. Inversely, if your primary employment is data analytics and your side hustle is as a milliner, it's unlikely that this side hustle work would fall under the IP agreement.

DOI: 10.4324/9781032689623-4

Scope of Employment: This section of the agreement defines the type of work and/or projects covered. If you are concerned about the murkiness of ownership of work when your side hustle runs parallel to your primary employment, this is the section that will help define what protections are already built in. Scope limits (or broadens) just how much IP the employer can recharacterize as their own based on what is laid out in this section.

Inventions and Discoveries: This section is particularly relevant to those filing for patents, copyrights, and the like. Some agreements will specifically address inventions and require a prompt disclosure, indicating that all inventions during the time of employment belong to the employer.

Non-Disclosure and Confidentiality: This section is the most straightforward and essentially prohibits sharing confidential information, trade secrets, or proprietary knowledge both during and after employment, sometimes for a set period and sometimes indefinitely.

Employee's Previous Work: If this section is included in your IP agreement, this is the carve-out provisions where you can specifically list IP created prior to employment that you explicitly want documented as set apart from your employment agreement. Employers also will clarify that they do not claim ownership of pre-existing work if this section is included.

Competing Work: Some IP agreements may specifically mention a non-compete or a prohibition from engaging in competitive work or activities that could be detrimental to the employer's business. Enforceability of this section will vary based on state, industry, and evolutions in noncompete enforcement as outlined in the preceding chapter.

After understanding and evaluating the agreement you may have signed with your employer, you must continue to take steps to define your rights and responsibilities concerning the creation and ownership of intellectual property during the course of employment. As a side hustler, it is important to safeguard your ideas, inventions, and creative works. Beyond the agreement itself, you should understand the following.

Types of Intellectual Property: Depending on the type of work you do, intellectual property can take various forms, including patents, trademarks, copyrights, and trade secrets. Your side hustle can have trade secrets! If you are innovating in an industry in a way that changes that industry materially, your innovations are trade secrets. For example, Uber's driver matching and route prediction technology were initially trade secrets within the ride hailing and taxi industries. The founders of Uber were involved in other companies and developed Uber as a side project, yet those trade secrets would go on to be the foundation of a company worth billions. Understand which category of IP your own work falls under to determine the appropriate protection strategy.

Registering for IP Protection: Depending on the type of IP, consider registering for patents, trademarks, or copyrights. This step offers legal protection and prevents others from using, making, or selling your intellectual property without your permission. For example, when writing my previous book, I registered for a copyright for the written work itself and a trademark for the title (which I planned to use beyond just the title, including for consulting and education purposes).

Implement Security Measures: This is a good step regardless of what you are creating or how far you are into your side hustle journey. It is important to protect your digital assets and sensitive information online through robust cybersecurity measures, including firewalls, encryption, secure networks, and regular software updates. Use a password manager, create and store your IP in a secure place, and protect the back-end of your side hustle too, through banking and conducting accounting with secure tools.

Monitor Online Usage: It is not enough to register your IP for protection or store it in a secure place. You must also regularly monitor online platforms, social media, and other digital channels to identify any unauthorized use of your intellectual property. You can use automated tools and services to help you monitor and protect your digital content. If you've ever received a "copyright strike" on Instagram or Tiktok for using a particular song or audio, you've experienced IP protection! It is important to regularly monitor the use of your intellectual property to identify any unauthorized usage or infringement. Equally critical is taking legal action as necessary against any infringement to protect your rights and deter future violations.

Conduct Regular Audits: Perform regular audits to assess any potential vulnerabilities in your IP protection strategies. This will help you identify and address any weak points that might leave your intellectual property exposed. You can also use online tools to help with audits, as many password managers will assess for weak passwords and many online reputation management tools will scan the internet for your personal or professional information. Even something as simple as a Google Alert can help identify any leaks of your information.

Consult Legal Experts: While all of the steps listed here can be done using online tools, it is also important to seek advice from legal professionals specializing in intellectual property to ensure you are taking all necessary steps to protect your intellectual property. They can provide guidance on the best practices and legal actions to take in case of infringement. Especially if your IP is created through a side hustle, having a legal expert to advise on specific additional steps based on your situation can help tremendously.

By implementing these steps, you can significantly improve the protection of your intellectual property at work and online. However, it's important to stay informed about the latest developments in intellectual property laws and regulations to ensure your protection strategies remain up to date.

To Consider:

1. What intellectual property do you already have that might need protecting?
2. What legal steps can you take to protect your intellectual property and how do these steps vary across different types of intellectual property?
3. How does your employer view your intellectual property?

Chapter 4

What Is Overemployment, and Is It Worth the Risk?

Landing your first "grown up" job in corporate America can feel like a bit of a rush. The salary—maybe it's finally enough for that apartment you've had bookmarked on Zillow for ages, or maybe it's at least enough for the handbag that's been screaming your name since you first got that targeted Instagram ad. Maybe you'll be able to afford a place that's all your own, or finally buy new clothes that don't directly reflect just how many years you've owned them. The job title—on paper, it probably feels more important than it actually is, insinuating more power than you actually have.

But after a while, that initial gloss starts to fade, the golden trappings of your new occupation begin to lose their luster. Maybe your lifestyle expands to the capacity that the salary permits, or those that you are supporting have new expenses that you need to cover. Suddenly, it's no longer enough.

Maybe the job never even paid enough to begin with—but you have student loans to pay and any job is better than no job.

And then Reddit tells you about this thing called overemployment and how it might just be the answer to your problems. Or you pick up a part time job whose hours balloon into a whole new 9–5 responsibility.

Suddenly, you're overemployed.

If you're lucky, you're one of those whose overemployment paychecks fall on the opposite Friday of your regular job's payday, making every Friday a magical day as thousands of dollars trickle into your bank account like clockwork.

And if you're reading this wondering what kind of sorcery allows every Friday to result in a multi-thousand-dollar payday, let me back up and explain.

What Is Overemployment, Exactly?

Overemployment is a modern-day gold mine, a high risk—high reward endeavor that unsurprisingly started within the technology industry. The movement (yes, it's a movement) encourages subscribers to maximize

DOI: 10.4324/9781032689623-5

income by holding multiple remote jobs simultaneously. The word itself comes from excess too—workers have more jobs or more income than they actually need (or more than a typical full-time employee would have).

Practically speaking, overemployment works best if you are a remote employee. If you're remote and salaried, you likely have the flexibility of both time and schedule that allow you to best maximize multiple jobs. To accomplish this, you schedule meetings around each other and sometimes work only partially-overlapping hours (say, 7–3 and 9–5) to minimize conflict, all the while keeping coworkers and managers in the dark.

With the rise in popularity of "quiet quitting," overemployment becomes easier still. Quiet quitting is a misnomer for simply doing your job's expectations—no more, no less. By eliminating the extra work that is often uncompensated and unrewarded, it's often easy to complete the expectations of your role in less than 40 hours a week. Suddenly, two full time jobs don't take 80 hours a week, instead taking 60—the number of hours you were probably working before you "quiet quit." (Or, if leaving the banking or legal industries, you swap one 80–100-hour work week for two 30-hour work weeks netting double the pay.)

Isn't That Risky?

On its face, holding two full time jobs at the same time is risky. What about your resume? Your LinkedIn? The background check for your second job? What about interacting with coworkers socially? What if a coworker at Company A is married to a coworker in Company B? Not impossible, especially if both jobs are in the same industry.

Overemployed experts have you covered—each concern mentioned has an "easy solution."

- Only list the most prestigious company or role on your current resume.
- Make your LinkedIn private or deactivate it—if employers ask, you can say you just don't need a LinkedIn right now, as you're gainfully employed.
- Take your first overemployment role while at your current company—it's only natural for a current employer to show on a background check. This only becomes a problem if a third role is taken in the pursuit of overemployment (yes, there are people currently holding three full time roles at one time).
- If you're a remote employee, many social interactions of yesteryear don't happen as naturally. Whether you are or not, manage your social interactions with care to avoid just this sort of situation.

The legalities of overemployment were my first question when I heard about the movement—what about noncompete agreements or tax laws?

Specifically within the United States, employment is "at-will," meaning a free market exists. Concern only arises if a noncompete agreement mentions competitors, competitive activity, or conducting the same work for two employers or two separate financial gains. Many overemployed individuals will consult an employment attorney before beginning their second role. Working multiple jobs in the same industry is the most likely example of where an issue will arise here, especially if one or both roles are client-facing (where arguments of poaching or dual representation might occur).

Taxation is the trickier issue.

Generally, employers calculate tax withholdings based on W4 inputs and overall assumed salary for the year. A salary of $100,000 at a single company versus two separate $100,000 salaries will result in different tax bills versus withholdings. This can be partially mitigated by having each employer withhold extra or by saving money on the backend to manage the end of year tax bill, but be advised that penalties do exist for underwithholding.

401ks also complicate things. Most employers automatically shut off 401k contributions (or switch to post-tax contributions) once you hit the annual federal limit. This mechanism doesn't exist when your annual limit is being spread across two companies, especially if one has a more favorable match than the other. An overemployed worker will need to diligently track, manage, and adjust for 401k contributions outside of any official employer mechanisms to avoid contributing beyond the limit.

That's a Lot of Work: Why Do It?

It's true—managing and navigating overemployment can be a full-time job in and of itself. The reason most proponents of the overemployment movement do it is for the financial gains. A single $100,000 salary is nothing to scoff at, but two six-figure salaries for one human? That sort of money can be life changing for any number of people. Especially when factoring additional income, company stock, 401k matches, and other financial benefits that can be acquired twice over.[1]

Overemployment is different from more traditional side hustles in a few ways:

Table 4.1 Comparison of Overemployment and Side Hustles

	Overemployment	Day Job + Side Hustle
Money	Two stable salaries, often two sets of RSUs, two end of year bonuses	One stable salary, second income is dependent on business performance and expenses (i.e. variable too).

	Overemployment	Day Job + Side Hustle
Effort	While holding two full time jobs at the same time isn't no effort, it can actually involve working just 40–60 hours a week by managing expectations.	The adage "quit a full-time job working for The Man to work two for myself" rings true— side hustles take work to set up, work to sustain, and work to execute. Often more than "just" 10–20 hours a week.
Thought Leader-ship	Discussing the second (or "overemployed") job is a big no-no, so any industry influence gained from that work is often invisible.	Side hustles are a more "acceptable" form of thought leadership so any industry influence can be used at work or in other places that outside influence is considered.
Costs	To be safe, overemployment often necessitates a formal CPA relationship and sometimes retaining an employment attorney as well. These costs are not as easily tax deductible.	Side hustle expenses can be planned for and managed, and often are deductible against income, reducing the tax liability that comes from the secondary income.
Mental Health	"Keeping a secret" 24/7, even from those close to you, can impact mental health in a tremendously negative way.	While still impactful to mental health, the downsides of a side hustle can be more easily protected through boundary setting or intentional business planning.
Social Relation-ships	It would be nearly impossible to have social friends at the second (or "overemployed") job without causing some possible exposure of the "massive secret."	Many social relationships built through side hustling have a sense of grit and endurance to them, through the perseverance necessary to build a business. These relationships are often life-lasting.
Stress Levels	While overemployment can be stressful for various reasons, there is much to be said for "someone else setting the direction" in both roles being held, requiring less strategic thought from the overemployed worker than it might otherwise.	Side hustling and self-employment are stressful, and side hustle burnout is such a common phenomenon that it has 1.2M hits on Google. Ditching a side hustle[2] is more common than ditching overemployment, primarily for stress related reasons. Stress can also lead to lack of consistency, which diminishes overall income and benefits.[3]

In the end, it is up to the individual to make the decision on whether overemployment or a side hustle will net the most balanced and impactful outcome to their personal and financial bottom line. What matters most is having an exit strategy—a contingency plan for when the financial benefits of your primary employment go bottoms-up.

To Consider:

1. Does overemployment or side hustling make more sense for my situation?
2. Have I fully evaluated all of the factors that impact my selection?
3. Do I understand the complexities of my selection that will impact my financial and professional life?

Notes

1 https://www.bbc.com/worklife/article/20210927-the-overemployed-workers-juggling-remote-jobs.
2 https://www.forbes.com/sites/ryanrobinson/2018/10/16/side-hustle-burnout/?sh=663c4fba7e7a.
3 https://www.vox.com/even-better/23317604/side-hustle-burnout-work.

Part II

Navigating the Workplace

Chapter 5

Selling Your Side Hustle as an Advantage at Work

If you're engaging in any sort of side hustle, it's only natural to want that side hustle to bolster your corporate professional life in some way. Organizing the outcomes and skills gained from your side hustle to communicate at work can be a strategic and meaningful way to showcase the myriad of positives that come from juggling multiple pursuits. As employers increasingly hire for skills like "intrapreneurship" or the ability to build an entrepreneurial pursuit within a corporate organization. If you plan to package and sell your side hustle as an advantage at work, there are a few things to consider to ensure that you're not accidentally opening yourself up to policy violations or other issues.

Selling your side hustle as an advantage at work is different from leveraging your side hustle to build a career and these two topics have been separated into two chapters as a result. Selling your side hustle requires structuring the work that you are doing in a way that someone in your leadership chain can get on board and validate what you've sold. Leveraging your side hustle to build your career is a step that "answers to no one" as you are instead using your side hustle to build the life you want versus in a way that serves someone else's goals.

Before making the decision to sell your side hustle as an advantage, first ensure that you **understand your company's policies**. Review the employee handbook and other documents you might have been given during onboarding or can retrieve from the company's HR portal. Specifically look for language around external projects and businesses, employee intellectual property, noncompete or nonsolicitation policies, and what the company defines as a conflict of interest. Having a clear understanding of how your company defines each of these components will empower you to sell the advantages you've gained without treading awry of policies that might cause you to be fired.

Ways to Sell Your Side Hustle as an Advantage

Once you understand the scope within which you might highlight your side hustle's advantages, consider taking one or more of the following steps to demonstrate the strength of your work.

DOI: 10.4324/9781032689623-7

The easiest way to turn your side hustle into an advantage at work is through **identifying transferable skills**. While we'll also discuss this in the next chapter as it relates to building your career as a whole, identifying transferable skills can help you in your current role too, even if you are not looking to secure a new role or opportunity. Take a moment to identify the skills you've acquired through your side hustle that are applicable to your current job. Think creatively and even consider both your side hustle and current job through an outsider's perspective. These transferable skills can then be used in your current job to unlock opportunities to improve performance, grow within the scope of your role, or even do work that will result in a bonus!

Even if you're not looking to expand your scope of role or get promoted, by **highlighting achievements** from your side hustle that relate back to your current job, you can create opportunities for yourself within your corporate role! You can showcase notable achievements that demonstrate your expertise and thought leadership. Do this by using concrete data, such as increased visibility from a recent book launch, positive customer feedback from a major client, or successful/highly visible projects, to emphasize your impact.

Whether you are identifying transferable skills or highlighting achievements, ensure that your communications are **aligned with company goals**. Keep these goals top of mind and frame your side hustle in a way that aligns with your company's objectives. Ensure that you are highlighting how your entrepreneurial experience has enhanced your understanding of the industry, market trends, or customer needs relevant to your company. This alignment will help your manager and leadership team make sense of how your side hustle connects to your current job.

If your side hustle can be aligned to the team or organization in a way that **shares knowledge**, this can also make it tremendously useful to the organization, and therefore more valuable. For example, in my recent time working in staffing, it was painfully clear that much of the team was not familiar with data analytics, scripting, SQL, or even complex spreadsheet formulas. In my side hustle as a book influencer (talking about new release titles on social media), I leverage a complex spreadsheet to track the 450+ books I have read this year. I was able to share more about my side hustle (which then made me the go-to book recommender on the team) and also help the team upskill on a few key spreadsheet formulas, as well as importing database information into spreadsheets. This equipped the team with more data on their own work, and eventually expanded to neighboring teams, and became a key point in my end of year performance review highlighting my team-wide thought leadership and impact.

You also might be able to highlight your **time management, efficiency,** and **productivity skills** that come naturally from juggling multiple priorities. In addition to my core employment, I work seasonally as a tax manager within Intuit TurboTax, managing a team of 35+ employees during the tax season. While many of my manager peers work exclusively at TurboTax during the season (one manager works during tax season and travels the rest of the year, another photographs weddings the rest of the year, etc.), TurboTax is actually a side hustle for me. One of the only ways to make this sustainable is through the use of automations and efficiencies. Some of the initiatives I launched within my team ended up saving so much time and reducing stress that they've been expanded to other teams. These include:

- Slack automations for repetitive tasks, such as weekly timesheet reminders or answering frequently asked questions through keywords. (For example, I have a Slack automation set to reply with home internet reimbursement instructions whenever someone in my team posts in our team slack channel asking about "internet reimbursement.")
- Surveys upfront to collect key ongoing information. (For example, I ask my team through a survey about their preferences for team meetings, 1:1s, recognition, and more. This frees up our 1:1 conversations for more critical content such as career goals or performance expectations.)
- Offline review options for when team members miss meetings. (Instead of going over team meeting content in a 1:1, I share the slides and my notes in a Google Drive folder and team members review offline and then complete a quick Google Form indicating they've done so, thereby giving them credit for having "attended" the meeting.)

These efficiencies in my side hustle have shown up in my core employment as well. After seeing the immense aid that Slack automations offer, I have also learned how to use automation bots within Google Chat in my day job. I have also highlighted various opportunities for asynchronous dissemination of information similar to the "offline review" for team meetings, thereby not only creating efficiencies but also offering content in more formats thereby supporting more learning styles. In both my side hustle at TurboTax and my core employment, I am seen as a productivity and automation expert, when in all reality it was the need for efficiency to juggle both that developed this skill.

Take a Step Back: Identify Your Advantage

If, after reading through these opportunities, you're wondering what your side hustle's advantage might actually be, that's okay! Identifying your unique skills (and therefore your side hustle's advantage) is a valuable process that can help you understand your strengths and how you might "stand out from the crowd" in various aspects of life, especially your career. Take some time to try one or more of the following.

Self-Reflection: It is important to create space for self-reflection to consider your past experiences and the tasks, activities, or accomplishments that you enjoyed and/or excelled in. The "and/or" is critical here—sometimes there are skills that we excel at that are not necessarily enjoyable, and sometimes there are things we enjoy but are not proficient in. Also take time to reflect on feedback you have received from others regarding strengths or accomplishments.

Feedback From Others: Beyond specific feedback on strengths that you might have already received, consider asking colleagues, friends, mentors, or family members what they think you might be great at beyond what you already do. It is not uncommon for others to see strengths in us that we might not recognize ourselves. If possible, ask for specific instances or examples where they believe you have excelled or had a unique contribution, or for them to highlight specific skills that they believe might lead to future accomplishments.

Leverage Skill and Personality Assessment Tools: If a more analytical approach is helpful to you, take advantage of the various skill assessment tools and personality tests available online. These tools can help you identify your strengths, weaknesses, and preferences that might aid in highlighting your unique advantage. These tests include StrengthsFinder, Myers-Briggs Type Indicator (MBTI), the DISC assessment, and many others. If you choose to use these assessments, they should only be one part of your overall exploration and not the primary research tool, but can still provide additional insights.

Review Your Past Accomplishments: Take some time to look back at your past accomplishments and consider the skills and abilities you used to achieve those goals. Identify patterns, if any, in the tasks or projects you enjoyed and excelled in. Looking back in this way can reveal the skills that come naturally to you and help you showcase your unique abilities.

Still Hungry for More?

Consider engaging in **skill development and exploration**. If after identifying your advantage and selling it at work, you are seeking additional opportunities to demonstrate your value, you can develop your "edge skills" or net-new skills. (Edge skills are those that might be strengths if developed just a little further.)

To do this, actively engage in new experiences and challenges to discover your strengths. Take on tasks that you haven't tried before and pay attention to the aspects you find enjoyable and where you excel. Experimenting with new skills in this way allows you to identify areas where you have a natural aptitude and passion.

Remember that identifying your unique skills is an ongoing process. As you evolve personally and professionally, your skills may also change. Regularly reassessing and updating your understanding of your strengths can help you make more informed decisions about your career and personal development. That said, by effectively communicating the value of your side hustle, you can position yourself as a valuable asset to your company, showcasing your diverse skill set and commitment to personal and professional development.

To Consider:

1. Do my side hustle and current job role share any traits or have any possible transferable skills?
2. If yes, can any of these skills enhance my performance and contribute to the growth of your career within your company?
3. Can I align any of my side hustle accomplishments to my company's objectives or goals? If I can, who should I share these accomplishments with?

Chapter 6

Leveraging Your Side Hustle to Build a Career

If you've been in corporate America for long enough, you know that the prevailing wisdom is to keep work at work and to keep everything else separate. Not many people talk about their side hustles or extra projects at work—you'd likely be surprised to learn that your deskmate is a part-time milliner or that the engineer four rows down is also a wedding photographer. You'll also be familiar with the notion that all the "extra stuff" you do at work is generally obligatory (i.e. if you don't do it, you're going to get the side eye or get passed over for opportunities) but it's not actually measured or rewarded in any meaningful way. All in all, if it's not your core work or responsibilities, the assumption is that it can't really impact your career growth or earning potential.

I'm here to tell you that not only is that prevailing wisdom wrong (or more accurately, it's a thing of the past that some people still cling to), but your side hustle has way more power than you ever realized—it can even make or break your career. Side hustles are this weird nebulous territory where a little bit of marketing and a splash of storytelling can change the game entirely. Don't believe me? Let me explain.

I've worked at Google for the last five years and nearly all of that was in sales. While I have outside education and consulting experience in HR, prior to 2021 I had absolutely zero corporate HR experience. Despite this, I was ready and really wanted to transition to a career in HR. I knew from past experience and watching my peers' career trajectories that an internal transfer was going to be a lot easier than getting a net-new HR job at a new company.

I redid my resume, repositioned my sales roles so that the transferable skills that carried over to HR were a lot more obvious, and started applying to internal HR roles. In March 2021, I interviewed for a sourcer job (part of the staffing world within HR) and in June 2021, I began that new role as a sourcer. I was able to explain the ways that I had gained sufficient experience in HR through consulting and my education to justify the transfer.

DOI: 10.4324/9781032689623-8

That seems pretty straightforward, but I then was able to take things one step further.

In May 2022, I heard from a recruiter at Amazon who was looking to hire for a staffing role that was significantly more senior than my current role at Google. The role required five to ten years of staffing experience, experience with client management (i.e. working in an "account manager" capacity with hiring managers on their open roles), and the capability to have significant influence and impact over recruiting delivery, even leading a team of sourcers. None of which were things I had corporate experience doing.

At the time that recruiter reached out, I had ten months of corporate staffing experience. And while I did have an advanced degree in HR, general HR studies cover employment laws and employee relations significantly more than they cover staffing concepts. So why did they believe I was qualified to even interview for a senior role in staffing? My decade-long consulting side hustle.

Repositioning Side Hustles for Corporate Success

If you have any form of side hustle, you're likely familiar with the amount of work that goes into it and the myriad of skills that you learn. You're not able to work solely on the thing that is your skillset—i.e. if you're a painter, having an artistic side hustle doesn't mean that you just paint and people magically buy your finished pieces when they're done. That side hustle likely also entails:

- Photography (capturing your finished pieces to share them in any format other than in-person, as well as for digitizing to make prints)
- Marketing (sharing about your finished pieces and maybe even your process, creating a brand for yourself as an artist, finding people online who like your work and want to buy originals or prints, convincing galleries to incorporate you into an upcoming show, running ads, figuring out SEO, running your social media)
- Operations (the day to day of running a business, managing all of the components you need, the "supply chain" of acquiring brushes/paint/canvases)
- IT (setting up an email, buying a domain and connecting it to your website, connecting the various tracking pixels to your website so you can later run ads, upgrading your wifi to manage business needs)
- Finance (annual income taxes, transactions for each sale, figuring out sales tax if relevant, bookkeeping, general work to make sure you turn a profit)

- Brand and web design (creating a logo or working with someone to create a logo, designing or outsourcing the design of a website, printing marketing materials, creating packaging for prints)
- Legal (creating or finding a website privacy policy, managing or finding contracts for commissions or corporate projects)
- Copywriting (every component of running and marketing your business requires writing—LOTS of it)

And many more things that I've likely forgotten to list here. While you might outsource some or all of these things as your side hustle grows, many individuals do all of these things when they're starting out in an effort to minimize business expenses.

The difference between you and someone who has a corporate full-time job as a painter or artist is that while they may dabble in these other components or sit in meetings with the folks managing those tasks, it's highly unlikely that they are navigating all of those tasks alone in addition to the actual art.

That difference sets you apart. In the same way that a liberal arts degree is touted as the best and most diverse skillset a student can graduate with,[1] the impact a side hustle can have on your skills as a corporate employee is beyond advantageous. If you're a marketer at work who has created a consumer good as a side hustle, you understand the consumer decision journey more fully than your colleagues who only experience product development in strategy conversations during marketing planning.

The ability to take these nuanced and plentiful components of your work as a side hustler and translate them back into saleable skills in your full-time job is the secret sauce to your long term career success. While your side hustle is mostly marketed online in an effort to sell the product or service you've created, the way you position your side hustle on your resume or LinkedIn should be near-fully focused on the skills that translate back to your corporate career.

Most side hustlers present their business on their resume and LinkedIn as follows:

[Functional title] at [Side Hustle Name]   Year-Present
I support [ideal client] by [service provided].
or I make [product] sold at [website or storefront].

For me, this would look like:

Lead Consultant at Focused on People   2008-Present
I support companies in shifting their HR practices to be people-first, increasing employee satisfaction, retention, and productivity.

It's not a bad way to list a side hustle. It is clear and to the point and gets at what is being made or sold, but doesn't do any favors when it comes to corporate career integration.

A better presentation might look like this:

Founder and Lead Consultant at Focused on People   2008-Present

CEO of a business focused on supporting companies in shifting their HR practices to be people-first, increasing employee satisfaction, retention, and productivity. Responsible for:

- Development and project management of client employee engagement strategies, including surveys, educational content, and diversity, equity, and inclusion initiatives.
- Creation and execution of custom workshops using proprietary solutions to overhaul corporate marketing + communication efforts.
- Managing internal team of employees, agency providers, and consultants, including hiring/firing, contract negotiation, performance reviews, employee relations, benefits management, retention, and flexible work situation crafting.

Immediately it becomes clear that my expertise is in HR but due to the nature of being a small business owner, there are other domains where I have gained significant expertise. For me, many of these translate directly into my corporate role as a sourcer as well, making the link between the two even more clear (while still differentiating where noncompete boundaries might lie). It still lacks the "outcome-based" ways that resumes should be formatted (i.e. "Accomplished [X] as measured by [Y], by doing [Z].") but clearly states the way my small business skills can and do translate into my corporate experience.

This can be made even better by using LinkedIn's formatting to include relevant media pieces or public-facing projects, or even by having a landing page on your website meant for corporate visitors. It also sets your work up to be better interpreted by LinkedIn Recruiter searches or searches run within applicant tracking systems. The first version names you as an entrepreneur but doesn't give you credit for that work in the searches that staffers run.

Circling Back to Google: Why Storytelling Matters

That Amazon opportunity wasn't the only time my side hustle has helped me get an interview or job offer. In fact, when I was interviewing for my first role at Google in 2017, I had zero corporate sales experience. When one of the interviewers asked me to explain a little about my sales background,

I flat-out responded that I actually didn't have any sales experience, my background was in marketing.

He looked at me a little dumbfounded and asked "well, how have you been putting food on the table for the past two years?" You see, for the two years prior to Google, I had been a mostly-full-time entrepreneur. And he was right—I wasn't paying my bills through magic or a bit of luck—I was selling my clients on why they needed to hire me, then delivering on the services I promised.

That interviewer changed my entire perspective on how I viewed and valued my side hustle, a change in perspective that has completely shifted my career and changed my ability to succeed in the workplace.

It's not enough to be able to translate your many side hustle skills and responsibilities into written formats for professional presentation. Once you land the interview, get the career transition opportunity, or need to share more about your side hustle at work, you need to be able to concisely explain why your side hustle matters.

Early in my career, I did this incredibly poorly. As a result, most of my employers had a negative perception of my side hustle—they saw it as a cash grab and diminished it through diminutive names like "Dannie International" that almost poked fun at what I was doing. They'd even ask me on Monday what my "little business" got up to over the weekend.

It was only after that pivotal conversation with the Google interviewer that I truly understood the power that my side hustle could have at work.

I made the proactive choice to change the way I positioned my side hustle. When I landed future interviews, I had specific examples (using the classic STAR interviewing method)[2] of the outcomes of my side hustle skills that might impact my corporate job. For example, in my second round of Google interviews, I had a sales example ready to go. I was able to talk about a time I'd had a difficult client in my side hustle and how I was able to problem-solve their issues, leverage customer service skills to get things back on track, and ultimately deliver what was promised. Those were all skills I'd eventually leverage in that first role at Google.

Think About Your Career, Not Your Job

Perhaps the most important part of side hustle positioning is recognizing that career trajectories today don't occur within the ecosystem of a single company. Your employer today is likely not the employer you will retire from in 40 years. However, your side hustle could produce ever-increasing income for you throughout the entire course of your career, as it is portable—it moves with you wherever you go.

We're often tempted to diminish our side hustle work, whether because of feedback from bosses or prevailing advice on social media. But the benefit of your side hustle extends far beyond the money it provides—it's an opportunity to build thought leadership that will have a profound impact on your corporate career, moving you up the ladder faster than through your full-time work alone.

I've been a side hustler for more than 15 years now. I've spoken at conferences, authored a book relevant to my side hustle work, and of course, built and maintained a client list over the duration of my business' existence. As a result, I often have the opportunity to be quoted in the media or used as a source for relevant industry content. This happens so frequently now that I actually have a line item in my 1:1 document with my corporate boss to reference any media mentions I've had in the past week. My entire leadership structure up to my vice president is aware that I'm frequently quoted in the media and I've even had the opportunity to consult with my VP on her own media voice. This sort of exposure is not an inherent part of my day job work, creating opportunities at work that only exist because of my side hustle.

Regardless of where I go next or how my career shifts, that history of thought leadership, media quotes, past speaking engagements, and relationships built with those far senior to me at work will continue to follow me. Those experiences may not have a direct influence on whether or not I get a promotion at work, but they mean that I have advocates of my work in rooms that I am not able to be in or conversations I am not privy to. That sort of impact transcends nearly any work product I could generate in my day-to-day corporate role.

To Consider:

1. What transferable skills do you have that transcend specific roles or companies?
2. What do you want the totality of your career to look like (beyond your current role)?
3. How can you craft a narrative from your own work experience?

Notes

1 https://www.forbes.com/sites/willarddix/2016/11/16/a-liberal-arts-degree-is-more-important-than-ever/.
2 The STAR interview method is a way to respond to interview questions concisely and meaningfully by discussing the specific situation, task, action, and result of the situation you are describing.

Chapter 7

HR Policies and Their Impact on Your Side Hustle

While previous chapters in this book have discussed intellectual property, noncompete, nonsolicitation (or no-poach), and confidentiality policies, you might be surprised to learn that there are a handful of other human resource (HR) policies that will impact your side hustle within the context of your day job as well.

The Impacts of Noncompete Agreements on HR Efforts

(And recommendations to HR managers)

HR managers have long struggled to author and execute employee policies that effectively navigate the complex business considerations of the growing side hustle industry.[1] As the practice of moonlighting has proliferated in the modern workforce since the early 2000s (and in the true sense of the word for nearly a century), moonlighters have begun to present issues for HR managers.[2] These issues include:

- A perceived decrease in employee motivation and productivity.
- Concerns around competitive activity and noncompete policies.
- Conflicts of interest.
- The use of company time, proprietary knowledge, and property.[3]

HR managers face challenges with the specifics of moonlighting noncompete policies and capturing all the impacts without veering into illegal territory.[4] The impact of these challenges manifests in cases like the recent National Labor Relations Board (NLRB) case where a noncompete policy was struck down for being overly prohibitive. Perhaps as a result, moonlighting has grown as a general practice without a correlated rise in appropriate and collaborative measures taken by HR managers and organizations.

HR managers are also confined by the emerging learnings that overly restrictive noncompete policies that negatively impact employees have

DOI: 10.4324/9781032689623-9

resulted in contentious employer-employee relations, a decrease in employee motivation and productivity, and retention issues.[5] The retention issues in particular cost companies billions of dollars per year in hiring and training replacement talent.[6] The problem's impact is wide-reaching, as more than 44 million U.S. workers have side hustles outside of their primary employment role.[7] Many HR managers do not have adequate employee moonlighting policies to reduce conflicts of interest.[8] Employers and employees cannot currently avoid the conflicts of interest that side hustlers present in the workplace. Court systems have struck down blanket noncompete policies for being too vague or broad. More specific policies governing employee expectations, specifically those that combat the significant "side effects" of side hustling, like employee productivity levels, will be necessary to impact the workplace.[9]

Current policies feature overreaching restrictions and inconsistently enforced policies on moonlighting that present HR challenges in the workplace. This inadequacy becomes even more pervasive within the technology industry and similar, as many tech startups have underfunded HR departments and many compensation and employee relations issues to contend with.

The reevaluation of HR policies has been an emerging topic of focus over the past five years.[10] As corporate strategy evolves and business practices become increasingly complex, HR policies should also advance. However, HR policy evaluations produce less value than corporate strategy reviews, so HR policies remain deprioritized for review.[11] Greater understanding regarding the perspectives and experiences of HR managers across these topic areas might aid in the enhanced development of HR policies that consider these emerging and developing needs.

Other HR Policies That Impact Your Side Hustle

Beyond the policies already addressed, as HR departments struggle to understand what their options are for overseeing side hustles, there are some policies already in place that impact your side hustle.

Code of Conduct Policy: A Code of Conduct policy can have various impacts on an employee's side hustle, depending on the specific provisions outlined in the policy. These could include:

- Professional image expectations, if the policy includes guidelines on what is expected both within and outside the workplace. (Similarly, reputation management—engaging in a side hustle that could negatively affect the employer's reputation may be subject to disciplinary action.)

- Use of company resources, as employees should be cautious not to use their employer's time, equipment, or other resources for their personal businesses unless explicitly allowed by company policy.
- Disclosure requirements, if the policy requires employees to disclose external business activities, including side hustles, to the employer.
- Non-discrimination, as employees should ensure that their side hustles do not involve activities that could be perceived as discriminatory or unfair, aligning with the company's values.

Time and Attendance Policies: If your employer has a stringent time and attendance policy, it will be even more critical to document your efforts as discussed in Chapter 2. You'll want to ensure that the separation between your core employment and side hustle is irrefutable. As well, a stringent time and attendance policy might mean that you choose <u>not</u> to work on your side hustle during your lunch hour.

Overtime and Working Hour Restrictions: While overtime and working hour restrictions are generally a good thing for work-life balance, depending on the way your core employer leverages these policies, they may impact your side hustle efforts. If you work in an industry where unexpected overtime can come up (and also be compulsory), it may impact the execution of your various side hustle responsibilities.

Social Media Policies: Companies often have social media policies that dictate how employees represent themselves online. Side hustles promoted on social media may need to adhere to these guidelines to avoid conflicts.

Insurance and Liability: Side hustles, especially if they involve activities with potential risks, may run into issues with the company's insurance coverage or liability policies. This also applies if your employer offers employee discounts—for example, if you take advantage of a rental car discount offered by your employer but your travel is for your side hustle, you may run into liability concerns should an accident or other issue arise.

As part of your administrative processes in managing your side hustle, you should plan to regularly refer to company policies to ensure that your side hustle remains in line with expectations and requirements.

To Consider:

1. What are my employer's HR policies and how do they apply to my side hustle?
2. How should I navigate social media and professional conduct policies in relation to promoting my side hustle?
3. Are there any disclosure requirements for side hustles, and how should I communicate about my entrepreneurial activities to the company?

Notes

1 Meijerink, J., & Keegan, A. (2019). Conceptualizing human resource management in the gig economy. *Journal of Managerial Psychology*, *34*(4), 214–232. https://doi.org/10.1108/JMP-07-2018-0277.

2 Meijerink, J., & Keegan, A. (2019).

3 Smith, A. (2018, June 11). *Moonlighting ban worded too broadly*. SHRM. https://www.shrm.org/resourcesandtools/legal-and-compliance/employment-law/pages/moonlighting-ban-worded-too-broadly.aspx.

4 Smith, A. (2018, June 11).

5 Aran, Y. (2018). Beyond covenants not to compete: Equilibrium in high-tech startup labor markets. *Stanford Law Review*, *70*(4), 1235–1294. https://law.stanford.edu/publications/beyond-covenants-not-to-compete-equilibrium-in-high-tech-startup-labor-markets/.

6 Whysall, Z., Owtram, M., & Brittain, S. (2019). The new talent management challenges of industry 4.0. *The Journal of Management Development*, *38*(2), 118–129. https://doi.org/10.1108/JMD-06-2018-0181.

7 Sessions, H., Nahrgang, J. D., Vaulont, M. J., Williams, R., & Bartels, A. L. (2021). Do the hustle! Empowerment from side-hustles and its effects on full-time work performance. *Academy of Management Journal*, *64*(1), 235–264. https://doi.org/10.5465/amj.2018.0164.

8 Colvin, A., & Shierholz, H. (2019, December 10). *Noncompete agreements: Ubiquitous, harmful to wages and to competition, and part of a growing trend of employers requiring workers to sign away their rights*. https://www.epi.org/publication/noncompete-agreements/.

9 Aydinliyim, L. E. (2020). The case for ethical noncompete agreements: Executives versus sandwich-makers. *Journal of Business Ethics*, 1–18. https://doi.org/10.1007/s10551-020-04570-w.

10 Xiu, L., Liang, X., Chen, Z., & Xu, W. (2017). Strategic flexibility, innovative HR practices, and firm performance: A moderated mediation model. *Personnel Review*, *46*(7), 1335–1357. https://doi.org/10.1108/PR-09-2016-0252.

11 Xie, Y., & Cooke, F. L. (2019). Quality and cost? The evolution of Walmart's business strategy and human resource policies and practices in China and their impact (1996–2017). *Human Resource Management*, *58*(5), 521–541. https://doi.org/10.1002/hrm.21931.

Chapter 8

Noncompetes as Barriers to Mobility

Background on Noncompete Policies

Noncompete policies are legally binding contracts between an employee and an employer wherein the employee agrees not to enter into competitive activity (or directly compete with) the employer during (and occasionally after) employment.[1] These policies can sometimes be extended to include non-solicit clauses and often have financial or legal consequences for violation.

Noncompete policies, also known as restrictive covenants, have existed in contract law dating back to 13th-century English common law.[2] However, a court ruling in 1711 created the basis for modern-day noncompete agreement enforceability. In the current United States, noncompete policies cover 18% of workers, primarily higher-wage workers in skilled industries.[3] The use of noncompete agreements may soon change in the United States, as Executive Order 14036 was signed in July 2021 to stop unfair use of noncompete and other agreements impacting worker mobility (Exec. Order No. 14036, 2021).

Noncompete policies are also a key component of moonlighting employees' experience, as they are often the singular document that will define the extent of the moonlighting employee's ability to conduct external work. Understanding the terminology and scope of a noncompete agreement empowers moonlighting employees to discern which of their extra-employment activities might be considered competitive. Connecting with supervisors and HR departments is also necessary for operating within the bounds of a noncompete policy, if deemed to be enforceable.[4]

Noncompete Policies and Mobility

When enforceable, noncompete policies can serve as a severe restriction on career mobility, impacting earning potential, career growth, and the ability to leave a company (or not). These agreements can act as barriers to career

DOI: 10.4324/9781032689623-10

mobility by restricting employees from working for competing companies or starting their own businesses in the same industry for a specified period of time, or within a certain geographical area after leaving their current employer. As the enforceability of noncompete agreements continues to evolve, it is important to understand the most significant impacts of noncompete policies on career mobility:

Limiting Job Opportunities: Noncompete agreements can limit an employee's ability to pursue job opportunities with other companies in the same industry. This can reduce the number of available positions for the individual, particularly if the industry is concentrated with a few major corporations holding the majority of revenue or job opportunities.

Geographical Restrictions: Noncompete agreements often include restrictions on where employees can work after leaving their current position. This can be especially problematic for individuals who want to relocate or work in a different city or region, or inversely can force an employee to move in order to secure a new role.

Industry Specialization: Some noncompete agreements are so specific that they restrict employees from working in a particular niche or sector within an industry. This can significantly limit an individual's career options, especially if they have expertise in a specific area.

Entrepreneurial Constraints: Noncompete clauses can also restrict an individual's ability to start their own business in the same industry. This can be a significant barrier for entrepreneurs who want to use their skills and knowledge to create new ventures.

Stifling Innovation: Noncompete agreements may discourage employees from pursuing innovative ideas or projects within their current company if they fear it might limit their future career options. This can stifle creativity and potentially hinder the company's overall innovation.

Negotiating Power: Employees may feel compelled to accept less favorable terms or stay in positions that are not aligned with their career goals due to the fear of facing legal consequences if they violate a noncompete agreement.

Reducing Wage Bargaining Power: With limited options for employment in a specific industry or region, employees may have less bargaining power when it comes to negotiating salary and benefits. This can lead to lower wages and less favorable working conditions.

Legal Costs and Uncertainty: Challenging the enforceability of a noncompete agreement can be costly and time-consuming. Many employees may opt not to pursue legal action due to the financial burden and uncertainty of the outcome.

It's worth noting that the enforceability of noncompete agreements varies by jurisdiction, and some regions have stricter regulations or may not enforce such agreements at all. In recent years, there has been increased scrutiny and debate over the use of noncompete agreements, with some jurisdictions considering or implementing reforms to strike a balance between protecting employers' interests and ensuring employee mobility.

Two Types of Career Mobility

While we frequently think about "the ability to find a new job" as the primary type of career mobility, another impact to career mobility is employers that do make space for side hustles. Because support for side hustles is currently tremendously rare, if an employee does build a successful side hustle, it may be difficult to eventually leave that employer knowing that support for the side hustle will not be as strong in other organizations. This can create an inverse sort of restriction, where instead of the concern being "where might I go," instead the concern is "have I lost all my bargaining power because I feel I have to stay." This inverse restriction introduces a unique dynamic where the perceived obligation to remain with a supportive employer may, paradoxically, limit the very career mobility one seeks. The dilemma extends beyond job hunting, encapsulating a delicate balance between personal entrepreneurial pursuits and the security offered by a supportive professional environment.

This restriction or inability to leave can actually impact an individual's career in much the same ways that noncompetes restrict leaving an organization. For example:

Employee Disengagement: When employees perceive limited opportunities for career growth, they may become disengaged and less motivated. The lack of a clear career path can lead to a sense of stagnation, reducing enthusiasm for work and diminishing overall job satisfaction. If an employee feels they cannot leave due to "good support" for their side hustle, other parts of their career may suffer.

Skill Stagnation: Limited career advancement opportunities can hinder the development of new skills and capabilities. Without the prospect of taking on more challenging roles or responsibilities, employees may not invest as much in their professional development, potentially leading to a workforce with outdated skills. While the employee may continue to gain new skills through their side hustle, stagnation in their core role may dramatically impact their career trajectory.

An employee may feel indebted to their employer for being supportive of their side hustle, but the indebtedness may have just as extreme impacts as the noncompete might have had.

Organizational Barriers Introduced by Noncompete Agreements

While noncompete agreements are designed to protect businesses, they can inadvertently harm employers as well. By limiting the pool of available talent, these contracts may hinder a company's ability to attract and retain skilled employees. Additionally, businesses operating in regions with strict enforcement of noncompetes may find it challenging to recruit top-tier professionals, as individuals may be reluctant to join a company with overly restrictive employment contracts.

Noncompetes may also contribute to a lack of employee loyalty. When employees feel restricted by a noncompete agreement, they may become disengaged or actively seek alternative employment options. This turnover can result in increased recruitment and training costs for the employer.

Noncompetes can also discourage innovation and entrepreneurship. Employees with innovative ideas or a desire to create their own ventures may be dissuaded from doing so due to the fear of legal repercussions. This stifling effect on creativity can have broader implications for industries that rely on continuous innovation. Collaboration and knowledge exchange between professionals in the same field are also crucial for industry advancement. Noncompetes, by limiting such collaboration, can hinder the collective progress of an industry.

To Consider:

1. Reflect on your feelings and experiences regarding noncompete agreements. Have you ever been subject to such an agreement, and if so, how did it influence your career choices and professional development?
2. Delve into the challenges and benefits of balancing a side hustle with a full-time job, especially when a noncompete agreement is in place. How do you manage the potential conflicts between pursuing your entrepreneurial ambitions and honoring your contractual obligations to your employer?
3. Consider the legal and ethical implications of engaging in a side hustle within your specific industry. How do noncompete agreements affect your willingness or ability to pursue independent projects?

Notes

1 Fisk, C. L. (2001). Working knowledge: Trade secrets, restrictive covenants in employment, and the rise of corporate intellectual property, 1800–1920. *SSRN Electronic Journal, 52*, 441–528. https://doi.org/10.2139/ssrn.262010
2 Blake, H. M. (1960). Employee agreements not to compete. *Harvard Law Review, 73*(4), 625. https://doi.org/10.2307/1338051

3 O'Brien, M. (2018, October 19). Perspective | Even janitors have non-competes now. Nobody is safe. *The Washington Post.* https://www.washingtonpost.com/business/2018/10/18/even-janitors-have-noncompetes-now-nobody-is-safe/.

4 Nahrgang, J., Sessions, H., Vaulont, M., & Bartels, A. (2020, March 18). Make your side hustle work. *Harvard Business Review.* https://hbr.org/2020/03/make-your-side-hustle-work

Part III

Why Your Side Hustle Matters

Chapter 9

The Democratization of Side Hustle Opportunities

Side hustling is deeply rooted in the history of labor and employment. Over the past two decades, access to side hustles has only increased as the economy, legal landscape, and democratization of technology all serve to level the playing field.

The Evolution of Side Hustling

The shift towards a digital economy, coupled with the proliferation of the internet, has had a profound impact on the democratization of moonlighting. Access to technology has empowered individuals from diverse backgrounds to leverage their skills and expertise through online platforms. This has not only provided an avenue for financial empowerment but has also catalyzed the growth of a new breed of entrepreneurs and freelancers. Furthermore, the rise of social media and digital marketing has facilitated the promotion and visibility of side hustles, allowing individuals to reach wider audiences and establish their personal brands, thereby fostering a culture of entrepreneurship and self-reliance.

The democratization of side hustle opportunities has also been facilitated by the emergence of various sharing economy platforms, such as Fiverr and Upwork. These platforms have revolutionized the way individuals can market their skills and services, transcending geographical boundaries and facilitating global connections between freelancers and clients. The convenience and accessibility of these platforms have democratized the process of finding and engaging in freelance work, empowering individuals to monetize their talents and expertise on their own terms. This has not only expanded the pool of available opportunities but has also fostered a culture of collaboration and innovation within the gig economy.

The evolving legal landscape, including the transformation of noncompete agreements at the state and national levels, has played a pivotal role in shaping the dynamics of moonlighting. Historically, noncompete agreements were used by employers to restrict employees from working

DOI: 10.4324/9781032689623-12

for competitors or engaging in similar lines of work. However, recent legal reforms and debates have aimed to strike a balance between protecting the interests of employers and fostering a more flexible and inclusive labor market. This has led to a reexamination of the restrictive nature of noncompete agreements, thereby enabling individuals to explore diverse employment opportunities without being unduly constrained by contractual obligations.

Moreover, the **socio-economic implications** of the democratization of moonlighting are multifaceted and truly profound. On one hand, the proliferation of side hustle opportunities has provided individuals with a means to generate supplemental income, thereby alleviating financial strain and enhancing economic resilience. This has been particularly significant in the context of economic downturns and the challenges posed by the COVID-19 pandemic, where traditional employment opportunities have become increasingly precarious. On the other hand, the rise of the gig economy has raised concerns about job security, the erosion of traditional labor rights, and the lack of comprehensive social protections for freelance workers.

The evolving nature of moonlighting has also had a profound impact on the traditional employment landscape. With an increasing number of individuals opting for freelance work and side hustles, employers have been compelled to adapt their recruitment and retention strategies to accommodate the changing expectations and preferences of the workforce. This has led to a paradigm shift in the employer-employee relationship, with a greater emphasis on flexibility, remote work options, and a more dynamic approach to talent acquisition. Additionally, the growing prominence of remote work and freelance opportunities has contributed to the decentralization of the labor market, with geographical barriers becoming less of a constraint for both employers and workers.

Finally, the democratization of moonlighting has **catalyzed a cultural shift**, fostering a spirit of entrepreneurship and innovation among individuals from diverse professional backgrounds. The accessibility of online resources and the proliferation of entrepreneurial support networks have empowered aspiring freelancers and solopreneurs to pursue their passion projects and turn their ideas into viable business ventures. This has led to the proliferation of a vibrant startup culture, characterized by a spirit of creativity, resilience, and adaptability. Moreover, the democratization of moonlighting has fostered a culture of continuous learning and skills development, as individuals strive to remain competitive in an increasingly dynamic and fast-paced global marketplace.

Impacts of Democratization

However, despite the myriad opportunities and benefits associated with the democratization of side hustle opportunities, there are also inherent challenges and risks that must be considered. The lack of comprehensive regulatory frameworks and social protections for freelance workers has exposed many individuals to precarious working conditions, unpredictable income streams, and a lack of access to essential benefits such as healthcare, retirement plans, and unemployment insurance. Additionally, the hyper-competitive nature of the gig economy has led to concerns about downward pressure on wages, exploitative working conditions, and the commodification of labor, thereby exacerbating existing socio-economic inequalities.

Policymakers, employers, HR departments, and stakeholders are all charged with collaborating to develop holistic and inclusive solutions that prioritize the well-being and financial security of freelance workers. As this evolution continues, this will likely involve the implementation of tailored regulatory frameworks that ensure fair compensation, access to benefits, and protection against exploitative practices. Moreover, fostering a culture of ethical entrepreneurship and responsible business practices within the gig economy is crucial to promoting a sustainable and equitable labor market.

Why Your Side Hustle Matters

Side hustles represent both freedom and being boxed into a corner. The democratization of income growth through secondary employment and entrepreneurial pursuits is a tremendous shift in the way we've always thought about the economy. However, side hustles have also made resting a privilege. Only those with the financial security to support themselves _and_ grow their long term wealth to have a secure retirement seem to be able to take advantage of rest.

On one hand, your side hustle is the tool that capitalizes these mechanisms of security for you and your family. On the other hand, your side hustle is a theft of rest, relaxation, and recovery from burnout. While there is no magical solution to this duality, awareness of it is a first step towards identifying the path that best fits your life and needs.

The democratization of side hustle opportunities represents a transformative shift in the modern labor market, driven by technological advancements, evolving legal frameworks, and changing socio-economic dynamics. The rise of the gig economy and the proliferation of sharing economy platforms have empowered individuals to explore diverse income-generating opportunities and pursue their professional aspirations on their own terms. While this phenomenon has opened new avenues for financial empowerment and entrepreneurial growth, it has also underscored the need for comprehensive regulatory reforms and social protections to safeguard the rights and well-being of freelance workers. By fostering a culture of responsible entrepreneurship, promoting inclusive labor practices, and prioritizing the holistic development of the workforce, society can harness the full potential of the democratization of moonlighting while ensuring a more equitable and sustainable future for all.

To Consider:

1. Reflect on the impact of digital platforms and technology in democratizing side hustle opportunities. How has the internet and gig economy platforms transformed the accessibility of part-time work and entrepreneurial ventures?
2. Explore your personal experiences of leveraging side hustle opportunities to enhance your financial well-being or pursue passion projects. How have these opportunities influenced your work-life balance, and what challenges or successes have you encountered in navigating the evolving landscape of non-traditional employment?
3. Consider the societal implications of the democratization of side hustle opportunities. How does the rise of flexible work impact traditional employment structures and job markets?

Chapter 10

Side Hustles as a Student Loan Debt Solution

Economic Context of Student Loans

Student loan debt levels have skyrocketed in the past two decades, creating decreased economic stability for recent generations post-graduation.[1] The increase in student loan debt has caused correlated decreases in family formation, marriage, retirement savings, home buying, and several other formative adulthood activities, leading young professionals to look for ways to reduce the debt load beyond what full-time employment income can provide. Supplemental income generated by side hustles, even at the cost of full-time job productivity, relieves a debt burden that prevents millennials from advancing other areas of their personal lives.[2]

The burgeoning crisis of student loan debt has cast a shadow over the trajectory of young professionals, raising profound concerns about their long-term financial security and overall well-being. A comprehensive understanding of the dynamics and implications of this crisis is essential to comprehend the significance of the role that side hustles play in addressing this pressing issue. The shift in societal norms and economic trends has fostered an environment in which the traditional means of financial stability and wealth accumulation, such as steady employment and prudent saving, no longer suffice to offset the financial strain incurred by the relentless increase in student loan debt. The traditional narrative of pursuing higher education as a means to secure a prosperous future has been overshadowed by the bleak reality of burdensome debt and constrained financial mobility. Consequently, the traditional notions of financial planning and wealth management are being redefined to accommodate the evolving needs and challenges faced by the contemporary generation of young professionals burdened by student loan debt. In this context, the concept of side hustles has emerged as a compelling and pragmatic approach to counterbalancing the adverse effects of mounting debt, providing a glimmer of hope for individuals seeking financial solace and stability amidst the prevailing economic uncertainties.

DOI: 10.4324/9781032689623-13

The phenomenon of side hustles represents a significant departure from the conventional understanding of employment, underscoring the growing significance of diversifying income streams and embracing unconventional avenues of financial empowerment. As the traditional labor market continues to grapple with uncertainties and structural limitations, the concept of side hustles has gained traction as a viable and adaptive response to the financial challenges posed by student loan debt. By engaging in supplementary income-generating activities outside the confines of traditional employment, individuals can harness their skills, interests, and entrepreneurial spirit to not only alleviate the financial burden imposed by student loan debt but also to foster a sense of autonomy and empowerment in their financial pursuits. Consequently, the adoption of side hustles as a pragmatic and proactive measure to counterbalance the adverse effects of student loan debt is indicative of a broader paradigm shift in the contemporary landscape of work, income generation, and financial sustainability.

Impact of Side Hustle Popularity on the Structure of Work

The surge in the popularity of side hustles has paved the way for a diverse array of entrepreneurial endeavors and innovative income-generating activities, thereby fostering a culture of creative entrepreneurship and financial resilience among individuals grappling with the repercussions of student loan debt. This burgeoning culture of entrepreneurship has engendered a newfound sense of agency and resourcefulness among young professionals, empowering them to proactively navigate the intricacies of the modern economic landscape and carve out their unique path to financial independence and stability. The rise of various online platforms and digital marketplaces has further facilitated the proliferation of side hustles, providing individuals with unprecedented access to a global audience and an extensive array of income-generating opportunities that transcend the limitations of traditional employment. Consequently, the democratization of income generation through side hustles has catalyzed a transformative shift in the way individuals perceive and pursue financial security, underscoring the transformative potential of embracing innovative and adaptive approaches to wealth accumulation and debt management in the contemporary era.

The pursuit of side hustles transcends the realm of mere financial necessity, encompassing a holistic approach to personal and professional development that empowers individuals to transcend the constraints of traditional employment and embrace a more dynamic and multifaceted approach to career advancement and self-actualization. By leveraging the flexibility and autonomy afforded by side hustles, individuals can harness their creative potential and entrepreneurial acumen to explore new avenues of professional growth and cultivate a sense of resilience and adaptability that transcends the limitations of conventional employment. As such, the cultivation of a vibrant and diversified portfolio of side hustles has emerged as a transformative strategy for individuals to not only alleviate the financial burden of student loan debt but also to foster a sense of purpose, fulfillment, and self-actualization in their professional endeavors.

The growing prevalence of side hustles has also instigated a paradigm shift in the traditional notions of work-life balance, prompting individuals to reevaluate their priorities, aspirations, and professional pursuits in light of the transformative opportunities presented by alternative income-generating activities. The conventional dichotomy between work and leisure is being redefined to accommodate the multifaceted demands and aspirations of a generation grappling with the enduring repercussions of student loan debt. In this context, the cultivation of a harmonious and sustainable work-life integration has emerged as a pivotal consideration for individuals seeking to strike a balance between their financial responsibilities and personal aspirations. By embracing the flexibility and autonomy inherent in the pursuit of side hustles, individuals can curate a personalized and adaptable work-life dynamic that fosters a sense of fulfillment, purpose, and holistic well-being, thereby transcending the confines of traditional employment and embracing a more nuanced and holistic approach to life and livelihood.

Impact of Side Hustle Popularity on Wealth Accumulation and Financial Empowerment

The proliferation of side hustles has engendered a paradigm shift in the traditional perceptions of financial empowerment and wealth accumulation, underscoring the transformative potential of embracing a multifaceted and dynamic approach to income generation and financial sustainability. As individuals navigate the complexities of student loan debt and the evolving landscape of work and employment, the cultivation of a diversified and adaptive portfolio of side hustles has emerged as a pragmatic and proactive strategy to counterbalance the financial strain and foster a sense of resilience and self-empowerment amidst the prevailing economic uncertainties.

By leveraging the opportunities presented by side hustles, individuals can cultivate a versatile and sustainable income stream that transcends the limitations of traditional employment, thereby facilitating a more robust and resilient financial foundation that fosters long-term stability and prosperity. As such, the transformative impact of side hustles on the contemporary landscape of financial empowerment and debt management underscores the enduring significance of embracing innovative and adaptive approaches to income generation and wealth accumulation in the face of burgeoning student loan debt and economic instability.

What This Means for Your Side Hustle

The escalating crisis of student loan debt has precipitated a profound shift in the contemporary landscape of financial stability and wealth accumulation, prompting the reconsideration of side hustles as a central and necessary tool for escaping student loan debt. As student loan payment resumes, many individuals are facing the return of a bill that has not been a part of their daily budget in more than three years, which prompts either (a) entirely reconsidering financial budgets and planning or (b) increasing income to absorb the increased payment responsibility. Faced with these choices, many individuals are choosing the latter.

When considering a side hustle as a possible tool for student loan debt repayment, it is important to ensure that:

1. The side hustle will generate more income than it incurs in expenses. (Prioritize opportunities that align with your skills, interests, and have the potential to contribute significantly to your debt repayment goals.)
2. Alternatively, if the side hustle operates at a loss, is it structured and executed intentionally as a business? (If not, the IRS will consider it "hobbyist income" and will not allow for the filing of a Schedule C and claiming business expenses against income.)
3. The side hustle is sustainable. (Is it a short-term gig, or does it have the potential for ongoing income? Sustainability ensures a consistent source of funds to address student loan debt and promotes a stable financial strategy.)
4. The side hustle is flexible both in a weekly and seasonal way. (This adaptability is crucial for accommodating your primary commitments and managing unforeseen changes in your schedule. A flexible side hustle allows you to maintain a healthy work-life balance while addressing financial goals.)

While side hustles are not a perfect solution to student loan debt, they are certainly an effective tool in generating additional income for monthly payments and offering the option to relieve some financial stress.

To Consider:

1. How does your side hustle align with your long-term financial objectives, especially in relation to paying off student loans?
2. How do you prioritize your time and energy between your primary employment, the side hustle, and managing student loan obligations?
3. How might your side hustle influence your perspective on financial independence and student loan debt?

Notes

1 Bozick, R., & Estacion, A. (2014). Do student loans delay marriage? Debt repayment and family formation in young adulthood. *Demographic Research, 30,* 1865–1891. https://doi.org/10.4054/DemRes.2014.30.69
2 Kuipers, P., & Wise, C. (2015). Are student loans hurting millennials? Despite justifiable concerns about the student loan bubble, millennials with loans that have recently entered repayment may represent an attractive target market. *The RMA Journal, 98*(4), 22.

Chapter 11

The Influence of COVID-19

COVID-19 had an outsize impact on side hustling and affiliated opportunities both positively and negatively. The work-from-home environment in knowledge-based industries has created an opportunity for new kinds of moonlighting activities.[1] There is now a sub-community of technology industry employees holding down two full-time jobs (overemployment), enabled by more control over their schedules and the absence of commuting.[2] And the resulting economic climate has created more income instability than we've known in recent years. The impact of COVID-19 can be summarized in six specific market factors influencing individual side hustles and the moonlighting economy as a whole.

Change in Demand

Some side hustles saw a dramatic rise in demand (such as grocery and food delivery) and others saw a dramatic decrease (such as ride sharing or in-home cleaning). These demand shifts impacted income generation and created massive shifts in personal safety and who was taking on risk. This change in demand presented both tremendous opportunity and tremendous harm for side hustle income generation. With many industries furloughing their employees, those side hustles with a rise in demand also had a willing workforce ready to meet the need.

For example, grocery delivery saw a massive increase in demand and was the side hustle industry with the largest number of adopters during the pandemic.[3] Those who were furloughed were able to not only apply for unemployment and the additional $300/week supplement, but also were able to tap into a side hustle offering significant payouts, especially for those who were able to shop multiple orders at the same time.

This change in demand also had a downstream effect impacting supply chains which then impacted side hustles. The publishing industry, for example, experienced a shortage of paper and an increase in production time for books, meaning that many books during the pandemic saw their early

DOI: 10.4324/9781032689623-14

success as eBook formats or on Kindle Unlimited. In a way, this democratized publishing modestly, as indie authors who publish on Kindle Unlimited saw a surge in reading both due to supply chain issues as well as the increased amount of time that people were spending at home.

Impact of Remote Work

Some side hustles that were able to operate remotely, such as freelance writing, virtual assistance, and online tutoring, saw increased demand as businesses and individuals sought digital solutions. This shift to remote work created opportunities for people with skills that could be utilized online.

The shift to remote work offered countless opportunities not only for improved personal lives[4] but also for employment and side hustle opportunities. As outlined in Chapter 4, the rise of overemployment and similar trends was enabled due to the mass-remote environment of the pandemic. As of August 2022, it was reported that 7.5 million workers (5% of the labor force), were working more than one job.[5] While it's complicated to evaluate the statistics specifically for those who are working more than one job during simultaneous hours, 5% of the workforce working more than one traditional job is significant.

Remote work also makes it easier to engage in a side hustle during the lunch hour or in time blocks that might have traditionally been used for commuting. This increased flexibility unlocks additional time for developing a side hustle that can generate meaningful and sustainable income.

Financial Instability

The economic uncertainty brought about by the pandemic forced some people to rely more heavily on their side hustles for income, especially if they lost their primary source of employment. This increased pressure to make ends meet through side gigs. While additional income has been one of the primary motivators for side hustles all along, it became the leading motivator during the pandemic.

Beyond just additional income, the importance of income diversification has become a central topic in the last four years as well. The massive numbers of furloughs and layoffs during the pandemic years led to an understanding that it is "safer" to have your income come from multiple smaller sources versus one large source. (I talk about my own income diversification in Chapter 1!)

Health and Safety Concerns

For side hustles that involved in-person interactions, such as dog walking, tutoring, or personal training, there were heightened health and safety concerns. Many individuals had to adjust their methods of service delivery to adhere to health guidelines, which often came with additional costs and complexities. This resulted in innovations or mass-availability of technology within existing sectors (such as zoom tutoring and online fitness classes) and the creation of new sectors to address health and safety concerns (countless Amazon shops popped up selling PPE throughout the pandemic and masks became their own industry). For example, would Touchland hand sanitizer have reached the mass-ubiquity it has today without the pandemic? While the company was founded more than a decade ago, it's only in the past few years that it's reached cult-following status.

Proliferation of New Sectors

The pandemic also created opportunities for side hustles in areas such as e-commerce, online content creation, and delivery services. The increased reliance on online shopping and home deliveries created a surge in demand for individuals with the skills to meet these needs. Entire new product lines and companies emerged, as did small creators.

For example, search "vaccine card holder" on Etsy or Amazon and there are now more than 2,000 results for a product that would have had very limited market appeal just five years ago. Similarly, while many people traveled with masks prior to COVID-19, there are now nearly 300,000 results for this product on Etsy, most of which reference language like "better protection" or "filter" today.

Finally, the number of companies that experienced explosive growth during the pandemic is impressive, although it is important to note that the reasons for their success were often specific to the unique circumstances of that time. Both Peloton and Zoom experienced mass market adoption during the pandemic, with Peloton even being able to IPO as a result of their success. Unity (video game) and DoorDash (food delivery) both IPO'ed in late 2020 after massive market gains in their respective industries. Palantir (data analytics) and Snowflake (cloud data warehousing) were two data companies who underwent IPOs in September 2020, both with massive success in early trading due to confidence in continued growth.

Economic Recovery Challenges

As the economy began to recover, the labor market faced challenges such as labor shortages and supply chain disruptions, which had ripple effects on various side hustles and gig economy jobs. Some sectors experienced a slower recovery, while others underwent significant transformations. Still today, the lasting impacts of COVID-19 can be felt in many individuals' decision to start or sustain a side hustle, as well as market reactions to increased income diversification.

Overall, the impact of COVID-19 on side hustling varied depending on the nature of the side gig and the ability to adapt to the changing economic landscape. Many individuals had to explore new avenues and develop additional skills to remain competitive in the evolving gig economy.

To Consider:

1. How has the demand for various side hustles shifted as a result of the COVID-19 pandemic?
2. How has the demand for various side hustles shifted as a result of the COVID-19 pandemic?
3. How have individuals adapted their side hustles to navigate the uncertainties brought about by the pandemic?

Notes

1 Feintzeig, R. (2021, August 13). These people who work from home have a secret: They have two jobs. *The Wall Street Journal.* https://www.wsj.com/articles/these-people-who-work-from-home-have-a-secret-they-have-two-jobs-1162886 6529.
2 Feintzeig, R. (2021, August 13).
3 Durbin, D. A. (2022, August 7). Demand for grocery delivery cools as food costs rise. *AP News.* https://apnews.com/article/grocery-delivery-service-demands-fall-d22c5424c235386ead5f344009540c4b.
4 Paköz, M. Z., & Kaya, N. (2023). Personal adaptations to remote working in the post-pandemic city and its potential impact on residential relocations: The case of Istanbul. *Transportation Research Record*, 03611981231174239. https://doi.org/10.1177/03611981231174239.
5 (2022). (rep.). THE EMPLOYMENT SITUATION—AUGUST 2022. Bureau of Labor Statistics, US Department of Labor.

Chapter 12

Thought Leadership and Social Media Influence as Financial Opportunities

While each chapter in this book has aimed to be simultaneously comprehensive and bite sized, this chapter will be the longest yet. The reason for this is that thought leadership and social media are one of the most universally accessible and most democratized side hustle opportunities that exist today. Thought leadership has also transcended both technology and time as a continuing source of income. "Visionaries of the moment" throughout history have built entire platforms and livelihoods through thought leadership, funding daily life, expeditions to the far corners of the globe, and everything in between.

Overview and Context

Social media influence has become an increasingly viable commercial activity in the past five years, paving the way for side hustles rooted in one's own knowledge and expertise.[1] Today, social media influencers are seen as viable human brands, and the ability to monetize one's own life creates an attractive side hustle. However, social media blurs the lines between employer activity and side hustling even more than other moonlighting activities.[2] One such example is the JLM Couture and Hayley Gutman lawsuit—Gutman signed over all legal rights to her name at the outset of her employment a decade ago.[3] Parallel to her employment at JLM, she built a social media brand for herself, which JLM is now suing for ownership of because they own her legal name.

Thought leadership and social media influence can also present nebulous noncompete challenges. While individuals own their own intellectual property, thoughts, and words, the gray area arises when some of that knowledge or language comes from employer-driven activities. Gutman is a talented wedding dress designer, but JLM's investment and promotional activities made her name high-profile enough for her to capitalize on other commercial activities. The increasingly blurred lines between who owns what

DOI: 10.4324/9781032689623-15

causes additional headaches, as contracts signed a decade ago could not have considered the power of social media today.

Thought Leadership Opportunities

Thought leadership has emerged as a powerful concept in the business world, transcending traditional marketing strategies and evolving into a significant financial opportunity for individuals and organizations alike. In the fast-paced and ever-changing landscape of industries, being recognized as a thought leader can provide numerous advantages, including enhanced credibility, increased visibility, and ultimately, financial success.

At its core, thought leadership involves positioning oneself or a company as an authority in a particular field by consistently producing valuable and insightful content. This content can take various forms, such as articles, blog posts, whitepapers, podcasts, or videos, and is disseminated through different channels like social media, industry conferences, and mainstream media. The goal is to offer unique perspectives, innovative ideas, and expert opinions that resonate with the target audience.

The financial opportunities tied to thought leadership are manifold. One of the primary benefits is the establishment of credibility. As a thought leader, individuals or organizations gain trust and respect within their industry. When stakeholders perceive someone as a reliable source of information and expertise, it opens doors to new opportunities, partnerships, and collaborations. This increased credibility can directly translate into financial gains, such as securing lucrative business deals, attracting high-value clients, or even commanding premium pricing for products and services.

Visibility is another key component of the financial potential tied to thought leadership. By consistently producing valuable content and engaging with the target audience, thought leaders can significantly expand their reach. This heightened visibility not only attracts potential clients but also catches the attention of media outlets, industry publications, and event organizers. Thought leaders often find themselves in demand as speakers at conferences, contributors to prestigious publications, or guests on influential podcasts. These opportunities not only enhance the individual's or organization's reputation but also provide avenues for additional income through speaking fees, writing engagements, and more.

Moreover, thought leadership can serve as a powerful marketing tool, reducing the need for traditional advertising and promotional efforts. When individuals or companies are recognized as thought leaders, their expertise becomes a magnet for clients and customers seeking solutions to their problems. This organic attraction can result in a more cost-effective and sustainable customer acquisition strategy, contributing directly to the bottom line.

In the digital age, where information is abundant, thought leadership becomes a way to cut through the noise and stand out in a crowded market. Being perceived as an authority allows individuals and organizations to differentiate themselves from competitors, creating a competitive advantage that can be leveraged for financial gain. This advantage extends beyond attracting customers to also include attracting top talent, investors, and strategic partners—all of which can contribute to the long-term financial success of a business.

To be clear, thought leadership is not just a buzzword; it represents a tangible financial opportunity for those who invest in building their expertise and sharing valuable insights with the world. Through increased credibility, visibility, and strategic positioning, thought leaders can unlock doors to new business opportunities, partnerships, and revenue streams. As industries continue to evolve, those who position themselves as thought leaders are likely to find themselves not only at the forefront of innovation but also reaping the financial rewards that come with being recognized as leaders in their respective fields.

Social Media Opportunities

Social media can both be considered a subset of traditional thought leadership and a wholly formed side hustle of its own, agnostic of industry expertise. In the digital age, social media has become more than just a means of communication; it's a powerful tool that, when leveraged effectively, can contribute significantly to revenue generation.

One of the primary financial opportunities presented by social media is the ability to reach and engage a vast audience. Platforms like Facebook, Instagram, TikTok, LinkedIn, and others offer a global stage to showcase nearly anything, from a product to an idea. By strategically utilizing these platforms, side hustlers can increase their visibility, extending far beyond traditional thought leadership, fostering a sense of community and loyalty that can translate into sustained financial success.

The direct monetization of social media platforms is another avenue for financial gain. Many platforms now offer features that enable the selling of products directly through their profiles. Instagram, for example, provides a "Shop" feature, allowing for showcasing and sell products within the app. Facebook and TikTok have similar platforms and "link-back" features.

Beyond selling ideas or products, influencer marketing is a burgeoning aspect of social media that offers unique financial opportunities. Influencers are individuals who have established credibility and a large following in a particular niche who are frequently contracted to promote businesses' products or services. The influencer's endorsement can significantly impact the purchasing decisions of their audience, resulting in increased brand awareness and sales for the business. Influencers are also able to charge fees for their services in addition to affiliate revenue shares or other agreements.

Niching Down: Specifics on Influencer Opportunities

Becoming a social media influencer has evolved from a trend to a lucrative financial opportunity, offering individuals the chance to monetize their online presence and interests. As the digital landscape expands, so do the avenues for influencers to capitalize on their personal brand and engagement with followers.

The primary financial opportunity for social media influencers lies in **brand partnerships** and collaborations. Companies eager to tap into the influencer's engaged audience are willing to pay for sponsored content, product placements, and endorsements. Compensation can range from free products to substantial monetary rewards, depending on the influencer's reach and niche.

Affiliate marketing is another avenue for influencers to generate income. By promoting products or services with affiliate links, influencers earn a commission for every sale generated through their unique link. This creates a symbiotic relationship where influencers benefit from their promotional efforts, and businesses gain access to a targeted and receptive audience.

Additionally, influencers can diversify their revenue streams through **exclusive content, paid memberships**, and **brand ambassadorships.** Exclusive content or premium subscription services allow influencers to provide additional value to their dedicated followers for a fee. Meanwhile, brand ambassadorships involve longer-term collaborations, often with regular content creation, establishing a more sustained income source.

Becoming a social media influencer is not just about amassing followers; it's about cultivating an engaged and loyal community. As influencers authentically share their interests and experiences, they not only gain financial opportunities but also the satisfaction of connecting with a like-minded audience. With dedication, creativity, and strategic positioning, becoming a social media influencer can translate into a rewarding and sustainable financial endeavor.

Types of Thought Leadership and Social Media Influence

There are a few different ways you can pursue thought leadership and social media influence, with varying impacts and time commitments. Here are some examples:

Table 12.1 Types of Thought Leadership

	Description	Impact
Original Written Online Content	Written online content can include LinkedIn articles, Substack or Medium newsletters, columns in publications like Forbes or Inc., email newsletters, or traditional blogs.	Initial setup of these platforms may take time, but once finished, they are wholly owned by the creator (except for columns) and can largely be monetized with tools like AdSense or subscriptions (for Medium and Substack).
Quotes and Media Contribu-tions	Providing frequent quotes to media using platforms like Help A Reporter Out (HARO) or Qwoted, which can then be reshared on social media once the links are live.	Low time commitment, easily discoverable, alerts can be set up based on areas of expertise. Can quickly garner a list of reputable publications that have quoted your expertise.
Social Media	Many platforms have platform-native attributions for thought leaders, such as "LinkedIn Top Voice." Posting regularly on a specific platform within an area of expertise can garner this recognition.	Not guaranteed and out of your control, limited recognition outside of the platform, however these tags are tremendously helpful within the platform itself for increased reach of your content. This may be helpful if you have off-platform products or services to sell.
Conferences and Events	Building a reputation as a strong public speaker can enable you to secure paid speaking engagements on the "conference circuit" within and proximately to your area of expertise.	Presenting at conferences, workshops, or industry events can position you as an expert in your field. Attendees and fellow speakers may recognize your expertise, and event organizers often share content from their conferences, extending your reach further.
Online Webinars and Workshops	Similar to conferences and events, you can use your own platforms to host free and paid workshops on topics you are an expert in.	Typically requires an existing audience if the workshops are paid, otherwise members of the public will be unlikely to sign up. However, recorded webinars are becoming increasingly common, where the replay is sold passively to online consumers, thereby reducing the time commitment necessary to derive income.
Publishing Books	Whether self or traditionally published, writing a book can help bolster your thought leadership and create opportunities for you to engage in other actions listed here, such as speaking at conferences.	High time investment, but could be an ongoing infinite passive revenue stream.
Adjunct Professor	Taking on an adjunct professor role at a university is a side hustle that also comes with a level of 1:1 impact that may be desirable to some.	Higher time commitment and lower pay, however, the personal impact can be significantly rewarding.

Real-Life Examples of Thought Leadership and Social Media Influence

As thought leadership and social media influence become increasingly common, here are a few real-life examples of side hustles and/or careers built from existing expertise.

A **registered dietitian** with a specific interest in the bariatric community built an educational platform and later a social media following based on real advice reflecting their own experience as a bariatric patient as well as experiences, advice, and guidance rooted in their medical expertise. [This individual eventually turned the platform into their full-time work.]

A **community building expert** with a passion for supporting marginalized humans built first side hustles and then a thought leadership platform around floral design and event production. Their work centers marginalized voices and prioritizes sustainable business practices.

An **HSN TV personality** with a love of crafts built both a side hustle and a thought leadership platform on crafting throughout the year as a way to bring people together, create community, and stave off loneliness. Over time, they wove their personal story into their platform, positioning them as the go-to voice where their three primary passions intersect.

A **customer engineer** with a passion for marginalized voices in tech started a side hustle writing code and building websites and eventually became a coding instructor, supporting others looking to break into tech in learning the necessary skills to do so. The motivation was both financial and impact-focused, enabling a special form of thought leadership that was rewarding in more ways than one.

All of these examples highlight the myriad of ways that thought leadership and social media can be integrated as a side hustle (and as primary employment, if desired). The upside to these forms of side hustling is that they translate well back into a primary career as well, as outlined in Chapters 5–6.

Connecting Thought Leadership to Corporate Employment

In the dynamic and competitive landscape of the modern workplace, thought leadership has emerged as a powerful tool for professionals seeking to advance their careers. Thought leadership goes beyond mere expertise; it involves actively contributing valuable insights, innovative ideas, and industry knowledge that sets an individual apart as a trusted authority in their field. The ability to position oneself as a thought leader can significantly impact career advancement in a day job. The examples shared here all have opportunities to connect their side hustle work back to their core employment and your thought leadership can too!

Thought leadership **enhances visibility and credibility** within an organization. When you consistently share well-researched perspectives and insights, you establish yourself as an authority in your domain. Colleagues and superiors take notice, recognizing your commitment to staying informed and contributing meaningfully to the intellectual capital of the organization. This heightened visibility can lead to increased opportunities for leadership roles, special projects, and participation in strategic initiatives.

Thought leadership **fosters a culture of collaboration** and idea-sharing. By actively engaging in conversations and discussions, you demonstrate your willingness to contribute to the collective success of the team. This collaborative spirit not only strengthens relationships with colleagues but also positions you as someone who adds value beyond the scope of your job description. As a result, you become a go-to person for input and insights, further solidifying your role as a thought leader within the organization.

Thought leaders are often seen as **problem solvers and innovators**. As you share your perspectives on industry trends, challenges, and potential solutions, you showcase your ability to think critically and strategically. This problem-solving mindset is highly attractive to employers seeking individuals who can drive positive change and contribute to the organization's growth. Consequently, your thought leadership can directly influence the decision-making process, increasing your chances of being considered for promotions and advancement opportunities.

The **networking benefits** of thought leadership should not be underestimated. By actively participating in industry events, webinars, and social media discussions, you expand your professional network. This network can be a valuable asset when seeking career advancement opportunities, whether within your current organization or through external job opportunities. Thought leaders often find themselves with a broader range of career options, as their reputation transcends the confines of their current job.

Thought leadership is a multifaceted strategy that can significantly impact career advancement in a day job. By enhancing visibility, credibility, fostering collaboration, showcasing problem-solving skills, and expanding professional networks, thought leaders position themselves as indispensable assets to their organizations, paving the way for continued success and progression in their careers.

Taking Small Steps to Get Started

If this chapter has felt overwhelming, know that building thought leadership is a gradual process that involves consistent effort and strategic actions. Taking any one of the following steps is a great place to start:

Identify Your Niche and Expertise: Determine the specific area or niche within your industry where you can demonstrate expertise. Focus on a topic that aligns with your passions, strengths, and the needs of your target audience (or company goals).

Engage in Industry Conversations: Actively participate in online discussions, forums, and social media groups relevant to your field. Share your insights, comment on others' posts, and contribute to conversations. This not only increases your visibility but also establishes you as someone in the know.

Network With Peers and Influencers: Attend industry events, conferences, and webinars to connect with others in your field. Engage in meaningful conversations, ask questions, and share your thoughts. Building relationships with both peers and influencers can amplify your reach and credibility.

Offer to Speak or Host Workshops: Volunteer to speak at company or local events, webinars, or workshops related to your expertise. Public speaking positions you as an authority and allows you to showcase your knowledge. Even small-scale events can be valuable for building your reputation and expanding your network.

The key to building thought leadership is consistency and authenticity. Over time, these small steps will contribute to a strong personal brand and help you stand out in your industry. As you gain recognition, you can gradually take on more significant thought leadership initiatives to further solidify your position as an industry expert.

To Consider:

1. Reflect on Your Niche Expertise: Consider your unique knowledge and experience in a specific niche or industry. How can you position yourself as a thought leader in this space?
2. Strategic Social Media Presence: Evaluate your current social media presence. How can you strategically leverage platforms like LinkedIn, Twitter, or Instagram to amplify your thought leadership?
3. Monetization Roadmap: Develop a roadmap for monetizing your thought leadership and social media influence. Explore various income streams such as sponsored content, speaking engagements, partnerships, and affiliate marketing. What steps can you take to attract financial opportunities while maintaining authenticity and providing value to your audience?

Notes

1 Ki, C., Cuevas, L. M., Chong, S. M., & Lim, H. (2020). Influencer marketing: Social media influencers as human brands attaching to followers and yielding

positive marketing results by fulfilling needs. *Journal of Retailing and Consumer Services, 55*, 102133. https://doi.org/10.1016/j.jretconser.2020.102133.

2 Nolan, E. (2021, May 6). Why JLM Couture is suing Hayley Paige Gutman for millions over her name. *Newsweek*. https://www.newsweek.com/jlm-cou ture-sues-hayley-paige-gutman-millions-over-her-name-1589140.

3 Nolan, E. (2021, May 6).

Part IV

Building Your Own Side Hustle

Chapter 13

Identifying the Right Opportunity

Throughout this book you've read about a variety of side hustles—my own, those that are commonly thought of, those that can extend throughout the life of your corporate career, and more. Hopefully, these ideas have sparked thoughts of what you might pursue as a side hustle, if you do not already have a concept identified. If not, or if you are looking to further refine your idea, this chapter will provide some foundational structure to assess your strengths and weaknesses to find side hustles that are complementary to but separate from your day job.

Your initial focus in launching a side hustle will depend on your own time availability, understanding of your skills and expertise, and types of work you are most comfortable with. To begin, you should be clear on the following:

1. *How much time do I plan to commit to my side hustle each week or month?* The less time available, the more the side hustle should be automated or passive to allow for time to be spent on administrative tasks alongside revenue production.
2. *Which of my skills am I most interested in monetizing?* What you are most skilled at may not always align with what you are most passionate about. Evaluate your skills based on reviewing your work experience, taking a skills inventory quiz online, or using a tool like StrengthsFinder.
3. *What type of work am I most comfortable with?* Do you want to be wholly responsible for the full operations of a business that you own? Would you prefer to primarily complete work for someone else and just be responsible for taxes and similar back-end components? Are you looking for something in between? Understand what elements of running a business you do and do not want to be responsible for.

In Chapter 12, we reviewed four steps you can take in building your thought leadership—these steps can also be applied to identifying the right opportunity for your side hustle in general. To recap, those four steps are to identify your niche and expertise, engage in industry conversations, network with

DOI: 10.4324/9781032689623-17

peers and influencers, and offer to speak or host workshops. These steps can be supplemental to your considerations after answering the three questions presented earlier.

Broad Types of Side Hustle

Table 13.1 indicates some broad types of side hustles, categorized as service- or product oriented, or skill-based. This table is meant to jumpstart some ideas for what you might consider pursuing, you may also consider a combination of these categories to create your own unique side hustle.

As you dive into defining what your side hustle will be, you can use this table to start to define what type makes the most sense for the time you have available to side hustle and the level of involvement you want with the business backend of things. You also can begin with one of these elements and then add additional elements as your side hustle begins to grow.

Testing Your Choice

If you are looking for an opportunity to test your business idea before it launches publicly or to a broader audience, consider a small beta test with friends and family or trusted colleagues. Beta testing is an important part of the development and launch of any new business. It involves releasing a prototype or early version of your offering to a limited group of users before the official launch. This approach allows you to gather valuable feedback, identify potential issues, and make necessary improvements, ultimately increasing the chances of a successful launch.

One of the primary benefits of beta testing is the opportunity to gain insights from real users. No matter how thorough internal testing may be, real-world users often encounter issues or have perspectives that the development team might not have considered. By exposing your business to a diverse group of beta testers, you can collect a range of feedback that goes beyond the expectations of your internal team. You also are able to confirm that you actually enjoy doing the work before you launch your business fully and commit publicly to taking on clients or selling products.

The early feedback obtained during beta testing can be invaluable in refining your product or service. Whether it's uncovering bugs, identifying user experience challenges, or discovering unmet needs, this information empowers your team to make informed adjustments. It's a chance to ensure that your business meets the expectations of your target audience and delivers a positive user experience.

Beta testing is actually a marketing tool in itself as well. Inviting users to be part of the beta testing phase creates a sense of exclusivity and involvement. People love being early adopters and having a say in shaping the final

Table 13.1 Types of Side Hustle

Type	Category	Definition and Examples
Freelancing	Service-Oriented	Offering your skills to others for a fee. Format includes listing skills on platforms like Upwork or Fiverr, contracting directly with other business owners, or creating and listing your work for sale online. Skills include: writing, graphic design, programming, online tutoring, virtual assistance, app development, ghostwriting, social media management, remote tech support, event planning, language translation, fitness coaching, life coaching, car detailing, and more.
Consulting	Service-Oriented	Offering your expertise to others for a fee. Format includes marketing your expertise and selling in time-based packages, flat-fee offerings, workshops, or via public speaking. Skills include areas like business, finance, career, or personal development.
E-Commerce	Product-Oriented	Selling products online through your own or another platform. Format includes creating and selling products, dropshipping products, or selling things you've already created (such as photography or graphic designs as prints or on products through third party platforms like Society6 or Casetify).
Affiliate Marketing	Service-Oriented	Promoting other people's products and earning a commission for each sale made through your unique affiliate link. This can be done through a blog, social media, or other online channels. Works best with established platforms that have existing reach. Can be a supplemental side hustle.
Investing	Skill-Based	Using money you have to generate additional income. Format includes day trading, real estate investing, and similar types of income generation.
App-Based	Service-Oriented	Leveraging third party gig apps to generate income. Format includes creating a profile on apps like Uber, Lyft, DoorDash, Rover, TaskRabbit, or similar apps to provide a service based on a skill or equipment you already have.
Education	Service-Oriented	Similar to consulting, sharing your expertise with others, however the fee might not come from the end consumer but instead from ads or another third party. Format includes podcasting, adjunct instructing, developing online courses, etc.
Writing	Skill-Based	While writing is represented in other rows, it can be a side hustle on its own. Format includes building a side hustle around writing, to include blogging, paid email newsletters (i.e. Substack), books (self or traditionally published), contributing to media articles, etc. Pairs well with an overall thought leadership, consulting, education, or freelance side hustle.
Seasonal/ Temporary Employment	Skill-Based	Seeking a secondary job based on seasonal or temporary availability—i.e. retail work during the holidays, tax preparation work from Jan-Apr, and so on.

product. This not only fosters a sense of community but can also generate buzz and anticipation around your business launch. Positive experiences during beta testing can turn participants into brand advocates who spread the word about your business.

To conduct an effective beta test, it's essential to define clear objectives and parameters. What are the specific aspects of your business that you want to test? Is it the functionality, user interface, or overall user satisfaction? Establishing clear goals will guide your beta testing process and help you collect meaningful data.

Choosing the right beta testers is equally crucial. Aim for a diverse group that represents your target audience. Consider factors such as demographics, location, and usage patterns. This diversity ensures that you receive feedback from various perspectives, making the testing process more comprehensive.

Communication is key throughout the beta testing phase. Provide clear instructions to your beta testers, outlining what you expect from them and how they can provide feedback. Encourage them to be honest and detailed in their assessments. Regular updates and prompt responses to their feedback help build trust and engagement.

Beta testing is a crucial step in the journey of launching a new business. It's a proactive approach that not only helps you identify and address potential issues but also engages your target audience early on. By leveraging the insights gained during beta testing, you can enhance your product or service, build anticipation, and increase the likelihood of a successful and well-received launch.

Imperfection is Key

Launching a side hustle or business will never occur within a silo of perfection. You'll need to tweak things after launch, you'll pivot your product or service down the road, and other things will evolve. What is most critical is to actually commit to the launch and execute against the goals and plan you have defined.

To Consider:

1. How can you align your passions and skills to create a business that reflects your authentic interests?
2. How can you address unmet needs through a business that provides value and solutions?
3. Are there untapped opportunities in growing sectors that align with your interests and skills?

Chapter 14

Early Steps to Getting Started

There are countless ways to start a side hustle, however, a consistent recommendation is to treat it like a business from the start. This is important for US-based tax reasons as well as to save from having to go back and implement revised processes once your side hustle is further down the road. This chapter details not only the formal and legal components of starting a business in the traditional sense but additional steps to think about for side hustles as well. This chapter is by no means comprehensive and each of these topics and tasks should be further researched based on your specific side hustle.

Idea Confirmation

Once your side hustle idea is confirmed, there are a few initial steps you'll need to take to ensure you're prepared to engage in side hustling.

Determine your time commitment. Determine in advance how much time per week or month you have to allocate to your side hustle. Create a consistent schedule for yourself and notify anyone who might need to know, such as partners, children, or other family/friends.

Check in with your employer. If your side hustle has no connection to your core employment, you can skip this step. However, if there is any perceived connection to your core employment, you'll want to check in with your employer's noncompete policy and code of conduct to ensure there are no notification steps you are obligated to take. You'll want to keep these policies handy for future reference.

Craft your business plan. At the bare minimum, craft a one-page business plan that specifies the problem you've identified, your unique solution (or what your business' value proposition will be), what your business model will be, who your target customers will be, and what sort of financials you are hoping to do and/or any financing you may need. Even if your side hustle is as simple as renting out an unused parking space through an app

DOI: 10.4324/9781032689623-18

like SpotHero, still plan for what you hope to make and what expenses you will incur.

Come up with a name. Don't stress too much about the initial business name you come up with, as you'll need a name for legal formation but can then file a "doing business as" for any consumer-facing business name you'll use down the road. This initial business name will be used on legal filings, in your state or country's small business database, and on the "back end" of all of your business processes (such as bank accounts, etc.).

Official Formation

These are the necessary steps to take to start your business from a legal, regulatory, and tax perspective. There are additional recommended steps here for your own protection.

Determine your formation structure. There are a few different business structures that you might consider, including sole proprietorship, partnership, LLC (limited liability company), or corporation. If you are launching your side hustle solo, you might consider an LLC for additional protections. If you are forming your side hustle with a friend or business partner, consider a partnership.

- **Sole Proprietorship:** Simplest form of business structure where a single individual owns and operates the business. Owner has complete control over decision-making and receives all profits but is also personally liable for business debts and legal issues. Easy to set up and has minimal regulatory requirements, making it suitable for small businesses with low risk and minimal complexity.
- **Partnership:** Involves two or more individuals who share ownership and management responsibilities. Two main types: general partnerships, where partners share equally in profits and liabilities, and limited partnerships, where some partners have limited liability. Relatively easy to establish, and profits and losses flow through to the partners' personal tax returns.
- **Corporation:** Separate legal entity from its owners (shareholders), providing the highest level of personal liability protection. Ownership is represented by shares of stock, and the corporation is managed by a board of directors. Shareholders are not typically personally liable for corporate debts. Subject to more complex regulations and formalities, including regular meetings, record-keeping, and reporting.
- **Limited Liability Company (LLC):** Combines elements of both a corporation and a partnership. It provides limited liability for its owners (members) while allowing flexibility in management and taxation.

Members are protected from personal liability, meaning their personal assets are generally not at risk for business debts. Popular for small to medium-sized businesses due to their flexibility and ease of formation, offering a balance of liability protection and operational simplicity.

Complete legal, financial, and regulatory steps. There are a number of "formal" steps necessary for the legal and financial creation of your business.

- Business formation
    - State or country business registration: Each US state or country has different business registration requirements. Visit your specific locality's small business website for instructions. Within the US, most states require an initial registration and sometimes a specific license registration (i.e. agricultural, beautician, medical, etc.).
    - EIN (employer identification number) registration: If in the US, you'll need to file for an EIN with the IRS (Internal Revenue Service). This number is used for tax and banking purposes.
    - State sales or use tax registration—applies if you will be selling physical products and/or opening a physical location.
- Business insurance: Consider securing business insurance to protect your business, yourself, and the products or services you may sell.
- Business bank account: It is critical that your personal and business finances be kept separate. Open a separate bank account (ideally specifically a business bank account) where all incoming funds will first be deposited and all expenses will be paid from.
- Accounting and financial management: From the beginning, consider an accounting tool (or at the very least a spreadsheet for tracking income and expenses) to make tax filing and any necessary annual financial statements easier to navigate.
- Also consider:
    - Business credit card: For better managing business expenses and/or to build a business credit profile and earn credit card rewards.
    - Registered agent: Registered agent services allow for a third party to serve as a business's official point of contact, thus enabling business owner privacy, as your home address and personal information will then not be listed in the publicly-available small business database. [For the future: this registered agent address can also be used in email marketing and other tools for the same privacy reason.]
    - Trademarks: If you have created a unique business name that you wish to further protect, or will operate in a highly competitive niche or industry, consider trademarking your business name or key phrases. Consult with an attorney to identify your options and next steps.

Marketing and Brand Identity

As you prepare to formally launch your business, you have the option to engage in a number of online platforms and tools to help market your business, depending on the sort of side hustle you will engage in.

App-Based or Third-Party Side Hustle. If engaging in a third part (3P) side hustle, marketing may be less necessary. If you are starting a side hustle on Uber, Fiverr, or Rover, much of your marketing and work will occur within that platform and you may not need external marketing.

Independent or Self-Started Side Hustle. If engaging in an independent side hustle separate from 3P platforms (or only using 3P platforms as a component of your work), consider the following marketing platform recommendations prior to launch. This is not a comprehensive list, but meant to spark brainstorming of a variety of marketing options.

- Email Marketing: Consider creating an email list on platforms such as ConvertKit, Mailchimp, or Substack to be able to reach out to customers you acquire over time.
- Social Media Marketing: Consider starting one or more social media profiles (as relevant to your business) to market your offerings. Do not feel pressured to launch a social media profile on every platform available, it is ok to niche down to just one or two platforms early on until you have a good understanding of where your customers thrive most.
- Website or other "digital home": Consider building a website or other digital home/hub to centralize all of the different digital components of your business.
- Paid advertising: There are a variety of paid advertising options across the web, consider these if relevant to your business.
- Traditional marketing:
  - Direct mail campaigns (brochures, flyers, etc.).
  - In-person events such as trade shows, fairs, farmers markets, etc.
  - Print advertising (magazines, newspapers, coupon books, billboards).
  - Broadcast advertising (podcasts, radio, and television).
  - Promotional merchandise (pens, keychains, tote bags, etc.).
  - Flyers and business cards.
  - Incentives (sales, giveaways, free trials, discounts for reviews or testimonials, etc.).

You will also need to determine if it is appropriate for you to develop a consumer-facing brand identity. If you are engaging in consulting or thought leadership, it may work for your business to operate under your name from the outset. If developing a product or other services, a brand identity may be more appropriate. Here are a few things to consider when evaluating whether you need a brand identity:

Early Stage: It's generally a good idea to start thinking about your brand identity in the early stages when you're thinking about the plans for your business. This includes defining your brand values, mission, and target audience. This foundational work will guide the development of your visual elements later on. Even if you opt not to have a visual brand identity at this stage, being clear on your values and mission are an important step to starting a business.

Before Launch: Ideally, you should have a solid brand identity in place before officially launching your business. This ensures that your messaging, logo, and overall brand image are consistent from the start.

Rebranding or Refocusing: If you're going through a significant change in your business, such as a rebranding or refocusing of your products/services, it's crucial to update your brand identity accordingly. This can help communicate the changes to your audience effectively. This also applies if you've casually side hustled in the past but are now changing your focus.

Expanding or Diversifying: If your business is expanding its offerings or entering new markets, it might be the right time to reassess and possibly update your brand identity to align with the new direction.

Consistency Across Platforms: If you're already operating but find inconsistencies in your branding across different platforms (website, social media, marketing materials), it's a sign that you need to work on your brand identity to create a unified and cohesive look.

Customer Feedback: Pay attention to customer feedback and market perceptions. If you notice confusion or a lack of understanding about your brand, it might be time to refine your brand identity to better communicate your values and offerings.

Remember that your brand identity is not just about the visual elements like logos and colors; it also encompasses your brand's personality, values, and the way you communicate with your audience. Developing a strong and cohesive brand identity helps create a memorable and trustworthy image for your business.

First Year of Business

In your first year of business, you'll start to identify the recurring tasks necessary for administrative success within your side hustle. These tasks will likely include the following. Turning this section into a reusable resource for yourself will help you in tracking and managing all of these tasks.

1. Bookkeeping and Financial Management:

   a. Recording income and expenses
   b. Invoicing clients or customers
   c. Tracking and managing receipts
   d. Reconciling bank statements
   e. Income tax and other tax filings

2. Legal and Compliance:

   a. Keeping track of business licenses and permits
   b. Ensuring compliance with local regulations
   c. Reviewing and updating contracts and agreements (including organizing and maintaining important documents, archiving and filing paperwork, and keeping track of contracts, agreements, and legal documents)
   d. Annual reporting

3. Customer Communication:

   a. Managing client relationships
   b. Collecting and addressing customer feedback

4. Market Research and Analysis:

   a. Monitoring industry trends
   b. Analyzing competitors
   c. Assessing evolving customer needs and preferences

5. Content Creation and Marketing:

   a. Developing and updating marketing materials
   b. Creating content for social media or a website
   c. Planning and executing marketing campaigns

6. Scheduling and Time Management

   a. Planning and scheduling tasks and projects
   b. Setting deadlines and milestones
   c. Managing your calendar and appointments

7. Inventory Management (if applicable):

   a. Monitoring and restocking inventory
   b. Tracking product or service usage
   c. Managing suppliers and orders

8. Technology and IT Management:

   a. Updating and maintaining software
   b. Backing up data regularly
   c. Managing cybersecurity and data privacy

9. Networking and Relationship Building:

   a. Attending industry events or networking opportunities
   b. Cultivating relationships with other businesses or professionals
   c. Collaborating with partners or affiliates

10. Performance Analysis and Reporting:

    a. Generating and analyzing business reports
    b. Assessing key performance indicators (KPIs)
    c. Making data-driven decisions for business improvement

11. Professional Development:

    a. Continuously learning and improving skills
    b. Staying updated on industry best practices
    c. Seeking out training or educational opportunities

Regularly reviewing and optimizing these tasks will contribute to the overall efficiency and success of your side hustle during its first year and beyond. Ensuring you've allocated time for these tasks will help ensure that your side hustle continues to thrive.

A Note on Taxation

If you are a US-based business, it is critical to think about taxation up front. It is a general best practice to set aside 30% of all income you generate in the course of a side hustle or other business to ensure you're prepared for any taxes due at the end of the year. Most side hustles will file a Schedule C form on individual taxes (unless you formed a corporation or partnership, where different steps may apply). A Schedule C is filed using both income and expenses to generate a net business income that is then taxable. Some business expenses to track for end of year deductions include (not comprehensive, all may not apply):

1. Advertising: Costs related to promoting your business, such as online advertising, print ads, and promotional materials.
2. Car and Truck Expenses: If you use your vehicle for business purposes, you can deduct expenses such as mileage, gas, insurance, and maintenance. Keep detailed records or consider using the standard mileage rate.

3. Commissions and Fees: Payments to individuals or companies for services rendered, such as commissions to salespeople or fees for professional services.

4. Contract Labor: Payments made to freelancers, consultants, or other businesses for services provided.

5. Depreciation: The gradual loss of value of your business assets over time. This can include equipment, vehicles, and other property used for your business.

6. Insurance: Premiums for business insurance coverage, including liability insurance, property insurance, and business interruption insurance.

7. Interest: Interest on business loans or other business-related interest expenses.

8. Legal and Professional Services: Fees paid to attorneys, accountants, and other professionals for services related to your business.

9. Office Expenses: Supplies, postage, and other consumables used in your business. This can also include rent or utilities for a dedicated office space.

10. Pension and Profit-Sharing Plans: Contributions to retirement plans for yourself and your employees.

11. Rent or Lease Payments: Payments for renting or leasing business property, equipment, or vehicles.

12. Repairs and Maintenance: Costs associated with maintaining and repairing business property and equipment.

13. Supplies: Costs of materials and supplies necessary for your business operations.

14. Taxes and Licenses: Business-related taxes, licenses, and permits.

15. Travel: Expenses related to business travel, including airfare, lodging, meals, and transportation.

16. Utilities: Payments for business-related utilities such as electricity, water, and internet.

17. Wages: Salaries, bonuses, and other forms of compensation paid to employees.

18. Home Office Deduction: If you use part of your home exclusively for business, you may be eligible for a home office deduction. This can include a portion of your rent or mortgage interest, property taxes, and utilities.

It's crucial to maintain accurate and detailed records of these expenses, including receipts and invoices. Proper record-keeping will not only help you during tax season but also provide a clear overview of your business's financial health. Be sure to consult with a tax professional to ensure that you're maximizing your deductions and complying with tax laws.

Ongoing Resources

There are a variety of ongoing resources available to you. Consider visiting, bookmarking, or engaging with the following:

- United States Small Business Administration
- Your state/city Chamber of Commerce (or the US Chamber of Commerce)
- Minority Business Development Agency
- Small Business Resources offered by the U.S. Department of the Treasury
- IRS Small Business Portal (support for tax questions)
- Member-based organizations such as:

  - National Association for the Self-Employed
  - National Business Association
  - National Federation of Independent Businesses
  - National Women's Business Council
  - Women's Business Enterprise National Council

- Small Business Development Centers and the Small Business Legislative Council
- SCORE (the "nation's largest network of volunteer business experts")
- Entrepreneurship podcasts, books, and blogs
- Incubators and programs offered by many businesses for small businesses
- Grant and funding programs frequently offered by banks and financial institutions

To Consider:

1. What steps have you already taken and what steps do you still need to take to form your side hustle?
2. Have you clearly defined the goals and objectives for your side hustle? Are they SMART (specific, measurable, achievable, relevant, and time-bound) goals?
3. Are there resources listed that you plan to research further? If so, schedule time and list what you plan to research.

Continuing Education

You've made it to the end of the book! This is not the time to put your pen down, put this book on the shelf, and never look at it again. Leverage the concepts you've learned here in your own side hustle or career advancement. Following are some resources to keep you going. While the resources that follow are not perfect or comprehensive, I have tried to prioritize intersectional perspectives wherever possible.

Books to Read

- *Side Hustle: From Idea to Income in 27 Days* by Chris Guillebeau
- *The $100 Startup: Reinvent the Way You Make a Living, Do What You Love, and Create a New Future* by Chris Guillebeau
- *The Lean Startup: How Today's Entrepreneurs Use Continuous Innovation to Create Radically Successful Businesses* by Eric Ries
- *Zero to One: Notes on Startups, or How to Build the Future* by Peter Thiel and Blake Masters
- *The 4-Hour Workweek: Escape 9–5, Live Anywhere, and Join the New Rich* by Timothy Ferriss
- *Crushing It!: How Great Entrepreneurs Build Their Business and Influence- and How You Can, Too* by Gary Vaynerchuk
- *The Art of the Start 2.0: The Time-Tested, Battle-Hardened Guide for Anyone Starting Anything* by Guy Kawasaki
- *Founders at Work: Stories of Startups' Early Days* by Jessica Livingston
- *Pivot: The Only Move That Matters Is Your Next One* by Jenny Blake
- *Reinventing You: Define Your Brand, Imagine Your Future* by Dorie Clark
- *The Startup of You: Adapt to the Future, Invest in Yourself, and Transform Your Career* by Reid Hoffman and Ben Casnocha
- *Originals: How Non-Conformists Move the World* by Adam Grant
- *Range: Why Generalists Triumph in a Specialized World* by David Epstein
- *What Works: A Comprehensive Framework to Change the Way We Approach Goal Setting* by Tara McMullin

Podcasts to Consider

- What Works with Tara McMullin
- The Prof G Pod with Scott Galloway
- The Tim Ferriss Show
- WorkLife with Adam Grant
- HR BESTIES

Newsletters to Subscribe To

- I Hate it Here by Hebba Youssef
- What Works by Tara McMullin
- Rolling in D'oh by Jenny Blake
- Debrief by Cece Xie
- Better Team Habits by Charlie Gilkey

About the Author

Dannie Lynn Fountain (Murphy) is a multipassionate human. By day, she's a disability accommodations program manager at Google, and by night she supports clients and brands with HR-focused diversity, equity, inclusion, and belonging (DEIB) strategies. Her focus is on expanding disability inclusion within DEIB efforts by equipping people with the tools to craft change within their own situations, regardless of their seniority at work or authority within their team. Dannie Lynn has been interviewed or quoted in the *New York Times*, *Harvard Business Review*, *Forbes*, *Bustle*, *Bloomberg*, *Business Insider*, *Cosmopolitan*, *Digiday*, *The Everygirl*, *Girlboss*, and more. She is also the founder of the #SideHustleGal movement and the "original" Side Hustle Gal.

Dannie Lynn resides in Seattle with her attorney wife and their cats Spensa and Reichs. Their dog Briggs passed while this book was in progress and his memory lives on in publication. When not working, Dannie Lynn is reading books and scrolling BookTok, traveling the world, swimming and rowing, or stirring up trouble.

You can connect further with Dannie Lynn on Instagram @dannielynnfountain or on her website, www.danniefountain.com.

Love This Book?

Don't forget to leave a review! Every review matters.

You can also:

Request a copy of this book at your local library.
Send a copy to a friend with your notes inside.
Encourage your workplace book club or your team to read this book and
    discuss.
Organize a panel to discuss and debate this book's contents.

I thank you endlessly.

Discussion Guide

Allow this guide to kickstart a conversation about *Keep Your Day Job* but don't let it block the conversation—follow your thoughts.

1. What are some of the most effective side hustles you've come across, and how do they differ from traditional part-time jobs?
2. How do you think side hustles contribute to the overall financial stability and security of individuals in today's economy?
3. In what ways can a side hustle be transformed into a full-time business? What are the challenges and opportunities associated with this transition?
4. How do side hustles impact work-life balance and overall well-being? Are there any strategies to maintain a healthy balance between side hustles and personal life?
5. What are some of the common misconceptions about side hustles, and how can individuals avoid falling into the trap of unrealistic expectations?
6. How does the emergence of the gig economy influence the growth and prevalence of side hustles? What implications does this have for the labor market?
7. What role do technological advancements play in the facilitation and diversification of side hustles? How do these advancements impact the way people approach earning extra income?
8. Can side hustles serve as a means for personal and professional development? How do individuals leverage their skills and interests through side hustles to pursue personal growth and career advancement?
9. How does the concept of passive income relate to side hustles, and what are some effective ways to generate passive income streams through these endeavors?
10. What are the ethical considerations associated with certain side hustles, such as those related to the sharing economy, and how can individuals ensure that their activities align with ethical standards and practices?

Index

Note: Page numbers in **bold** indicate tables on the corresponding page.

Printed in the United States
by Baker & Taylor Publisher Services